ACCESSING EDUCATION

effectively widening participation

Penny Jane Burke

Trentham Books

Stoke on Trent, UK and Sterling, USA

Trentham Books Limited

Westview House   22883 Quicksilver Drive
734 London Road   Sterling
Oakhill   VA 20166-2012
Stoke on Trent   USA
Staffordshire
England ST4 5NP

First published 2002

British Library Cataloguing-in-Publication Data
A catalogue record for this book is available from the
British Library

1 85856 255 4

Designed and typeset by Trentham Print Design Ltd., Chester and
printed in Great Britain by Cromwell Press Ltd., Wiltshire.

iv

Contents

Acknowledgements

This book was only made possible by the inspiring contributions of my access students. I extend my sincere appreciation to them.

I am enduringly thankful to Gillian Klein, who has provided invaluable editorial advice and encouragement in turning my doctoral thesis into this book. Her integrity and insight have been crucial in this process. I have also been greatly fortunate to have the guidance of Debbie Epstein, my supervisor and mentor. Debbie has been central to my intellectual development and for that I am always grateful. Thank you to Alison Kirton, Melanie Mauthner, Christine Lawler, Joy Magezis, Norma Williams and John Curran for their generous interest and advice and for taking time to read and comment on draft chapters of the book.

I am forever indebted to my lovely family who has tolerated the intensity of this project in our lives. Thank you to my wonderful partner, Metin Ahmet, who has given me endless encouragement in my work. My beloved sons, Matthew, Timur and Djemil, have been patient and understanding while I have been constantly busy reading, writing and thinking. Thank you also to my mother, father and brother, Jason, for their love and encouragement. Without the friendships of Jenefer Davys, Kally Pattard and Esme Madill, this book would not have been possible.

I would like to dedicate this book in loving memory to my late grandfather, Bernard O'Quinn, who took great pride and loving interest in my work and always did his utmost to support me in any way he could.

1
Introduction

> [Widening educational participation] is about developing a sustained critique of current rhetoric, developing a distinctive *social* theory of knowledge derived from a politically committed analysis and theory of power which leads to a form of pedagogy that is concerned to democratise knowledge making and learning, in ways that redefine the very parameters of what counts as...education. (Thompson, 2000: 10)

Introduction

> [*Returning to education*] *has shaped my life. It's given me so much independence, I feel so independent now. I feel like my own person.* (Vicky, 1999)

This book is about widening educational participation. It draws on an ethnographic study of 23 students returning to learning through various access courses provided at their local further education college in suburban England.

The book seeks to reclaim the radical politics associated with access education. Current policies and practices have undermined the commitment to combat the social inequalities that are institutionalised and reproduced within the academic world. I hope the book will contribute to the creation of interactive strategies for the critical education of marginalised groups. Collaboration is vital to the development of inclusive access education policies and practices. Effectively widening participation depends on explicitly addressing the experiences, practices and meanings of the students themselves.

Concepts in accessing education

I used certain poststructural concepts as analytical tools to make sense of the experiences and autobiographies of access students. This chapter explains how these concepts are used throughout the book.

Discourse is a central concept, signifying that knowledge and power are inextricably intertwined. Discourse represents the different sets of meanings that define and shape how we understand the social world and our relationship to it. It shows 'how knowledge can determine and define meaning, representations and reason' (Davies, Williams and Webb, 1997: 15). There are always many competing discourses, although some will be more dominant than others at a particular time. I use Gramsci's concept of **hegemony** to represent the processes and struggles by which a discourse becomes dominant and, as Foucault (1979, 1975, 1986) would put it, a 'regime of truth'. As subjects who are always positioned within available discourses, we discipline ourselves or regulate our behaviour through and against these various regimes of truth. How do the different hegemonic and marginal discourses of widening participation shape the experiences of students and the possibilities of and for access education?

I want to know how different discourses, such as neo-liberalism or radical feminism, perpetuate or challenge social inequalities and how access students, as subjects, are positioned and constituted through these discourses in contradictory ways. I hope to mobilise‧ **radical** discourses and subject positions that are empowering and emancipatory and which seek to destabilise unequal relations of power. By 'radical' I mean the discourses that challenge unequal social relations, combat social exclusion and create emancipatory change.

2

Poststructural theory offers the analytical tool of **deconstruction**. Deconstruction is about identifying the different and competing discourses operating in educational fields and then unpacking them to discover the values, ideologies and politics embedded in them. Deconstruction works towards disordering sets of assumptions and destabilising taken-for-granted truths. The task of deconstruction, as a 'strategy of displacement' (Lather, 1991:13), is to make ideology visible and to probe the complexity of contradictory meaning, desire and pleasure derivative of certain classed, gendered and racialised positions.

A feminist approach to deconstruction would work towards new critical discourses for social justice. I worked with students to deconstruct the dominant and marginal discourses of widening participation and access education. For example, the dominant discourse of neo-liberalism that has largely shaped policies for post-compulsory education positions access students as consumers taking up education for instrumental reasons only. This seldom fits or adequately addresses the motivations, needs and interests of access students and it constrains opportunities for critical education. We wanted to collaboratively reshape meanings of education in relation to the diverse backgrounds and perspectives of access students.

The dominant discourse of neo-liberalism is also central in the formation of identity, regulating 'non-standard' students as classed, (hetero)sexualised, gendered and racialised. **Subjectivity** represents the complex processes of identity formation. It embraces the inter-relation between the personal and social and 'the ways in which a person gives meaning to themselves, others and the world' (Davies and Banks, 1992: 2 cited in Jones, 1993: 158). The production of subjectivity is always an interactive, inconsistent and unstable process, interlaced with the social, cultural and discursive. Subjectivity reflects the interaction between inner and outer worlds 'in a self-reflexive analysis of the internalisation of an engendered self' (Hey, 1997: 125).

My own sense of subjectivity profoundly shaped my work, which grew from a passionate belief in widening educational opportunities.

I bring to it experiences of access and adult education, as a student, researcher, external moderator and teacher. These experiences led me to identify **pedagogy**, a theory of the processes of teaching and learning, as a central issue for widening educational participation. The book aims to develop collaborative approaches to pedagogy and research that work with and against difference, address complexity and context and remain committed to anti-classist, antiracist and anti-sexist classroom practices.

During the period of the ethnography (1997-2001) the radical agenda of access education was being overshadowed by central government's efforts to widen educational participation. The progressive rhetoric adopted by Labour resonates with the aims of access practitioners in a highly seductive way that has undermined critical interrogation of the discourse constructed through these policy developments. This new dominant discourse is embedded in a neo-liberal logic that serves to reproduce social, cultural and economic inequalities, while claiming to be against social exclusion. This discourse places standards and standardisation at the centre of focus, so that issues of pedagogy that are crucial to creating inclusive learning programmes are blocked. In consequence we must critically engage the wider contexts of burgeoning policy on widening educational participation in order to understand the autobiographies and micro experiences of the access students in this book.

The Autobiography of the question

I have written myself into the book as a co-participant of the research. The research process was complicated *and* enhanced by my position as a teacher researching her students, and as a woman juggling paid and unpaid work, trying to negotiate the patriarchal boundaries that separate the private and public realms of social life. I did not experience my research as a separate entity. My life as a mother, wife, grand-daughter, daughter, friend, teacher, student, external moderator and researcher all overlapped, clashed and reinforced each other in ways that are rarely written about or theorised in the academic world.

A researcher approaches and makes sense of her/his work according to a complex web of factors including subjectivity, current socio-economic conditions, and geographical, political and historical contexts. As Diane Reay observes, 'all research is in one way or another autobiographical or else the avoidance of autobiography' (Reay, 1998: 2). My research was influenced by my identification as a feminist, my subjectivity and the many other dynamics that determine my perspectives and identities, so I was drawn to the theories that resonate with my own experiences, values and beliefs. I found this in critical social research and feminism, both of which explicitly politicise research (Carspecken, 1996; Maynard and Purvis: 1994; Epstein, 1991, 1993; Harding, 1991). This book aims to develop access education that:

- opens spaces to deconstruct dominant discourses

- reveals and disrupts unequal power relations

- attempts to reconstruct radical discourses

The book is therefore fundamentally and explicitly political.

The project grew from my experiences of rebuilding my life through access education after surviving domestic violence. So I start from 'the autobiography of the question' (Miller, 1997: 4), which means:

> beginning with the story of [my] own interest in the question [I am] asking and planning to research into. From that initial story, [I] may move towards the mapping of [my] developing sense of the question's interest for [me] onto the history of more public kinds of attention to it. This becomes a way of historicising the questions [I am] addressing and of setting [my life] and educational history within contexts more capacious than [my] own. Theory becomes theories; historically contrived to address or explain particular questions; and we are all theorists. (*ibid.*)

My research also represents an 'intellectual biography' (Stanley, 1992), as my research questions changed through exposure to various different theoretical positions. Beverly Skeggs observes that our trajectory through theories and theorists is entwined with our autobiographies. '...The period in which research takes place, the social location of the researcher and access to theories is central to the motivations and framing of the research' (Skeggs, 1995b: 195). Certain theory speaks louder to me, and the reason I find some theories more convincing than others relates to my shifting location in the social world. As Skeggs explains:

> We are thus being continually positioned by and positioning our-selves in relation to theory. This is not just a case of what we read but who we talk to, our institutional location, what our colleagues read, which conferences we go to and sometimes how we feel at the time. (Skeggs, 1995b: 196)

My research on access education began as an undergraduate study-ing the experiences of mature women students, motivated by my support for and belief in the feminist goal to 'make the voices of women heard', and it was influenced by theories of gender socialisa-tion and patriarchal domination. This led to an MA in Women's Studies and Education, specifically intended to expand my research on access education. My MA dissertation about the policy and practice of women's access to education represents a pilot study for my doctoral research. The stages of my research interest in access education are visible in the book in terms of level of nuance and sophistication, and of theoretical orientations. Initially I asked ques-tions such as:

- How can we widen educational participation to include people invisible in our society?

- How can education serve to challenge and interrupt per-sistent divisions and inequalities within British society?

As I engaged with feminist poststructural theory, my focus shifted to questions about identity transformations in relation to access educa-tion. These included questions such as:

- How do access students experience their subjectivities as shifting, while simultaneously being repositioned through dominant discourses as classed, gendered, racialised and sexualised?

6

Such shifts in theoretical orientation, clearly shaping and trans-forming the research emphasis and approach, reinforce the idea that all research is indeed autobiographical. A key theme throughout this book is **autobiography**, appearing as a concept, a method of data collection and a methodological issue. The story of 'the self' is always a social story and always interacts and interconnects with the story of others (Stanley, 1992: Birch, 1998).

Autobiography
Concept: autobiography is socially constructed – interconnects with the stories of others
Method of Data Collection: collecting participants' life and educational stories
Methodological Issue: exploration of the social dynamics involved in constructing an autobiography for research purposes

Figure 1.A: Autobiography

Reconstructing radical politics for widening participation

This research examines post-compulsory education that explicitly aims to widen access to groups who have been socially and cul-turally excluded from educational participation. This has come to be known as the access movement, and is most celebrated for its esta-blishment of discrete courses across Britain named 'Access to Higher Education'[1]. Since 1978, the access movement has contri-buted significantly to the opening of educational opportunities to traditionally excluded groups (Williams,1997a). However, access has undergone dramatic cultural changes over the past decade, through formalisation, standardisation, incorporation, marketisation and centralisation (Kirton, 1999; Spours and Lucas, 1996; Lucas *et al*, 1997). The prevailing discourse of the New Right over the past fifteen years has penetrated the field of access education, slowly

7

undermining its commitment and relationship to issues of social equality and justice (Barr, 1999:13; Benn, Elliott and Whaley, 1998: 1). It therefore appears that access education has largely moved away from a radical politics of social justice to a neo-liberal politics of vocationalism, competition and individualism (Thompson, 2000: 7; Ryan, 2000: 45).

This book sets out to reclaim the radical politics associated with the access movement. Its eclectic conceptual framework embraces both feminist structural and poststructural theory. Feminist structural theory with its commitment to liberatory projects, provides a framework for research as **praxis** – theory that is shaped by action and grounded in the practical and the political (Lather, 1991:11-12). I also consider the possibility of liberatory research (Robinson, 1997), although feminist researchers and teachers must recognise the limitations of research and education as tools for social change and justice (Maynard, and Purvis, 1994). Poststructuralism helps explore the complexity of power relations, the multiplicity of subjectivity and the fluidity of culture (Flax, 1995; Hernandez, 1997). *Feminist* poststructuralism[2] develops poststructuralist theory, rejecting the tendency towards nominalism[3], and maintaining the importance of concepts such as 'gender' and 'class' through the concept of **positionality**, used by Alcoff (1988) to express two key points. Firstly that 'the concept of woman is a relational term identifiable only within a (constantly moving) context'. Secondly that 'the position women find themselves in can be actively utilised (rather than transcended) as a location for the construction of meaning' (Alcoff, 1988: 434). The concept of positionality suggests that women 'occupy a range of social and cultural positions simultaneously' (Kenway *et al*, 1994: 199).

Joining together the insights of feminist structural and poststructural theories helps to explore the complexity of the subject's relationship to the social world in terms of power, positionality and subjectivity. The 'post' in poststructural does not merely represent a theory *following* structuralism, but *builds on* the insights of structuralism.

8

The main aims of this book

One aim is to trace the shifting, contradictory and hegemonic discourses operating in the field of access education. This means deconstructing dominant discourses of widening educational participation and examining their impact on the policy and political contexts in which access education is firmly located. Among the questions the book raises are:

- What are the connections between critical discourses of access education and dominant discourses of widening educational participation, and how do they compare?

- How can we understand, analyse and deconstruct these discourses in relation to the experiences of access students?

- How do these discourses frame and shape the experiences of access students and the subject positions available to them?

A second aim is to examine the implications of participation in access education for the lives, experiences and identities of access students through their written and spoken autobiographies. The students are positioned at the centre of research on access education. It seems pointless to try to develop access education that claims to redress social inequalities in the academic world unless one makes the diverse backgrounds, interests, ideas and experiences of access students the starting point and continual point of reference for **reflexivity**. As a process of ongoing critical reflection, reflexivity involves paying close attention to how our values affect our work in the field and classroom. Questions in relation to autobiography and subjectivity are:

- What do the autobiographies of a small group of access students reveal about dominant discourses of widening educational participation?

- What impact does educational participation have on the lives, relationships and identities of these access students?

- How is subjectivity produced through the process of participating in access education?

9

The book explores issues of social transformation and justice. Its third aim is to consider the possible ways access education might open spaces for localised changes that address cultural *and* material social justice issues (Fraser, 1997). One example of cultural inequality is the privileging within academia of culture specific sets of knowledge that are claimed to be unbiased and objective. Material inequality is the unequal distribution of wealth that perpetuates the advantage of particular groups to participate in higher education. I draw on Fraser's thesis that a project for social justice requires both a politics of redistribution, informed by socialist-feminist theories, and a politics of recognition, drawing on the insights of feminist poststructuralism and its tool of deconstruction. The book raises questions about social justice:

- Can access education address the cultural and material inequalities located in the academic world?

- Can it challenge dominant discourses of widening educational participation that reinforce such social injustices?

- How might educational spaces be opened up to mobilise radical discourses and subject positions?

Finally the book contributes to developing collaborative approaches to research and pedagogy within the field of access education. My research created an experimental space to practise collaborative approaches to developing new forms of pedagogy and methodology for widening educational access.

Central themes and issues

Two central themes shape this book: the concern to develop collaborative approaches to research and pedagogy of access education and the competing discourses of widening educational participation. **Chapter Two** examines policy and political contexts that shape and constrain possibilities for widening participation. It outlines the history of access education, the local geographical contexts of the research and describes the courses under focus. I examine the discourses operating in access education, making links between national politics, discourses of widening educational participation and access education. The problems of a market approach for the policy and practice of widening participation are shown to reinforce poverty and exclusion and to reproduce unequal power relations.

Chapter Three examines the value of collaborative approaches to research on access education and considers the implications of my dual position as teacher and researcher. Flexibility and reflexivity are important in critical research that involves the insights of marginalised groups; the researcher and participants alter their methods and approaches according to the contexts, situations, subjects and discourses encountered through fluid research processes and relations.

Chapter Four places pedagogy at the centre of inquiry. Collaborative pedagogy is crucial to the project of access education and the development of inclusive learning. Drawing on theories of critical pedagogy, co-participants engage with its critiques and the dilemmas we experienced while attempting to put such theory into practice in the classroom. I also examine the discourse of widening educational participation as used by the Government in its vision of the 'learning age' and by access practitioners. Although there appears to be consensus over the need to widen participation, closer examination reveals a tension between the dominant discourse, which is concerned with standards and standardisation, and critical pedagogy, which draws on a vision of social change and justice.

The participants' autobiographies are full of accounts of intimidation and inferiority. Although access education seeks to include marginalised groups in learning, its location in the academic world often positions access students as inferior to 'standard' students. **Chapter Five** discusses how the hegemonic discourses in operation in formal educational institutions reconstruct access subjects across and within systems of inequity such as class and gender. Discourses of selectivity reinforce such constructions, and they are reinforced also through discourses of standards and standardisation and struggles over rights to access. Access students are produced as 'equal but different', yet their difference is measured against the 'normal' ('A' level) student.

Chapter Six focuses on the participants' representations of their educational experiences in relation to their shifting subjectivities. The implications of educational participation are explored in relation to the multiple discourses it presents to access students who often return to study in the desire for self-discovery. Educational participation may generate contradictory identities that cause fractures rather than closures and confusions rather than certainties. Learning may be experienced as liberating and at the same time oppressive, as access students interact with new ideas that challenge past identifications and securities.

Chapter Seven considers the ways in which radical discourses are resisted within access education, in light of my experiences as a feminist tutor and my students' experimentations with feminist subject positions. Micropolitics is used as an analytical tool to uncover the discursive and material struggle evoked by our attempts to develop critical and feminist praxis within the research institution. A close analysis of micro-politics reveals the subtle ways feminist subjects may be actively othered by those who attempt to regulate any deviations from established social norms through technologies of normalisation. Is it possible to mobilise radical discourses through the site of access education?

Chapter Eight draws the book together. It shows how central themes of collaboration and the discourses of widening participation contribute to theory and practice in relation to access. Collaborative approaches to understanding and developing new strategies for widening educational access are shown to be of central importance.

Notes
1. Access is given a capital 'A' when I discuss the specific Access to Higher Education programme, but a small 'a' when I am referring to an overall approach to widening participation in post-compulsory education.
2. As in all theoretical fields, feminist poststructuralism is plural and contains competing positions and explanations within it.
3. Nominalism I define as the poststructuralist tendency to reduce everything to a text, ignore the material realities of social life and to dismiss categories such as class, gender and race as mere fictions.

2

Accessing Education in Context

Current trends in adult education policy, theory and practice also require interrogation and caution. Stirred by the progressive tone of some Labour language, there is a danger that rhetorical assertions about the importance of widening participation, combating social exclusion and recognising social capital, for example, take too little account of the material, gendered, racialised and ideological context in which all these initiatives are located. (Thompson, 2000: 8)

Introduction

This chapter sets the scene for the book by putting the ethnography into context geographically, historically and politically and by describing the access courses at the centre of inquiry. Key policy documents are examined to reveal the competing discourses of widening participation. 'Discourse' helps to 'explain the working of power on behalf of specific interests and to analyse the opportunities for resistance to it' (Weedon, 1997: 41) Political contexts are analysed, using 'discourse' to uncover and interrogate the construction of competing meanings within the project of access education. The chapter begins with a brief history of access education and the early radical discourses of widening educational participation that carried an explicit political agenda.

Historical contexts

Competing discourses are in play within access education (Williams, 1997a: 42). Different social players, including politicians, access practitioners, educational managers and access students, have struggled to redefine and control the access education agenda. Two analytically distinct discourses are currently in circulation but these, as Williams (1997a: 42) points out, overlap, and access practitioners may subscribe to either (Benn and Burton, 1995).

The first discourse is associated with neo-liberal politics and is most recently articulated through policy documents and public statements. It is part of the Labour project to reform the welfare state and regenerate the national economy and has gained a hegemonic position since 1997. However, it also has origins in the earlier split within the access movement, when some members focused on the 'A levelisation of Access' (Stowell, 1992: 172 cited in Williams, 1997a: 43) and a 'meritocratic version of access' (Williams, 1997a: 45).

The second discourse is associated with radical politics and was motivated by the concern to transform higher education by placing marginalised groups at the centre of knowledge reconstruction. 'The access movement draws upon a radical approach to education which asks for a fundamental shift in the distribution of cultural capital' (Williams, 1997a: 43). There are particular pedagogical concerns embedded within this discourse that draw on critical and feminist theory. These include:

- a student centred approach to teaching and learning

- the negotiation with students about course content and pedagogy, encouraging students to follow their own interests, and

- community-led organisation of access courses. (Kennedy and Piette, 1991: 35)

The access movement was generally practitioner-led and located outside of central state sponsorship (Diamond, 1999; Corrigan, 1992). Provision was designed around student needs and led to experimental approaches to the organisation of the curriculum and the construction of courses in response to the needs of local communities (Diamond, 1999: 186; Maxwell, 1996: 112).

Access education is not here restricted to nationally recognised Access to Higher Education courses, although these constitute a significant proportion of the field of access education (Tight, 1993: 62-75). It refers also to adult educational programmes that demonstrate a serious commitment to the expansion of educational participation in British society. Additionally, I see it as committed to engaging groups who have been socially excluded from participating in and contributing to the reconstruction of knowledge and meaning, and this shaped my research aim to contribute to collaborative approaches to methodology and pedagogy within the field. Addressing difference, complexity and contextuality demonstrates the impossibility of discovering one universal 'good' approach to access education.

Local contexts

The case study focused on one Further Education College, which I've called Ford College[1]. The case study researcher:

> typically *observes* the characteristics of an individual unit – a child, a clique, a school or a community. The purpose of such observation is to probe deeply and to analyse intensely the multifarious phenomena that constitute the life cycle of the unit with a view to establishing generalisations about the wider population to which that unit belongs. (Cohen and Manion, 1985: 120, original emphasis)

Case studies that draw on ethnographic methods characteristically involve participant observation (Willis, 1981; Cohen and Manion, 1985) and this is true of my research. I also draw on feminist work focusing on participants' experiences of particular institutions (Reay, 1998; Skeggs, 1997; Hey, 1997; Epstein, 1991, 1993). Such work engages with the nuanced detail of the particular case, paying close attention to the varied and interconnected contexts that profoundly shape and complicate the dynamics of the research focus.

I was employed as a lecturer in the Department of Adult Education at Ford College, so was able to carry out participant observation. Ford College consists of two centres and I was based across both.

The college sites are in different local councils within one large county council, 'Woodley Borough' and 'Riverside District Council'. The two centres are close enough for students to attend classes at both, travelling regularly between the sites.

Woodley Borough is next to extensive woodlands on the boundaries of a metropolis. The constituency is predominately English white upper-working and middle class, although this is gradually changing as more ethnic minority groups move into the area from the city. Its proximity to the city has enabled people from African-Caribbean, Turkish and Asian communities to register at Ford College, but this applies more to younger cohorts of the student population than the adult cohorts I researched. The 1995 annual employment census estimated that there were some 24,200 jobs in the borough, over 75% in the service sector. Two thirds of the jobs in Woodley Borough are full-time; women take 80% of the part-time jobs. The current unemployment rate is among the highest in the county, with substantial long-term unemployment.

Riverside District Council has a rich natural and built heritage in market towns and village settlements and is predominately rural. The population is approximately 124,000, half of whom reside in the district's five main towns, and half in over 100 villages and hamlets across the district. Ford College is located across from the river in one of the historical towns controlled by the Conservative Party. The district is generally prosperous with higher than average earnings and most of the workforce hold full-time managerial, skilled or technical jobs. The district council has one of the lowest rates of unemployment in the county. Many of the women I researched were housewives supported by a 'breadwinner' husband.

As a full-time lecturer at Ford College my key role was 'Return to Study Programme Manager', a post I held for just over one academic year (August 1997 – October 1998). Before this I was a student there myself on the City and Guilds 7306 Adult and Further Education Teacher's Training course, and I did my teaching practice at the College, on 'A' level Sociology and Return to Study (September 1996-June 1997).

Course Title	Level	Description	Site	Study Mode	Progression Routes
Return to Study (Year One)	1/2	A first step back into learning, building study skills, self-reflection, self-confidence	Woodley and Riverside	Part-time (one 2 hour session plus the option of nine hours extra tuition per week)	The Learning Pathway, Access to HE, GCSE or 'A' levels
The Learning Pathway: A Part of the Return to Study Programme	2/3	Emphasis on expanding academic skills, developing critical thinking and analysis	Woodley and Riverside	Part-time (Same as Return to Study-Year One)	Access to HE, 'A' Levels, Higher Education
Access to Higher Education	2/3	Emphasis on preparation for entry to degree level study	Woodley and Riverside	Part-time and Full-time	Higher Education
Women's Studies	2/3	Emphasis on critical thinking and analysis; available as an option on Return to Study, the Learning Pathway and Access to HE	Woodley	Part-time (one 3 hour taught class per week)	Access to Higher Education or Higher Education

Figure 2.A: Access Courses at Ford College

In 1998 I was awarded a full-time ESRC studentship to complete my doctoral studies and I resigned from my permanent post at the College. I continued to teach part-time on Return to Study, Access to Higher Education and Women's Studies. These courses all to some degree shared the goals of access education, but each was differently organised (see figure 2.A).

Return to Study

Return to Study was created by a lecturer five years before I came to the College. It is a flexible programme that emphasises confidence, critical thinking and study skills. It consists of five units validated by the Open College Network plus other course options, including GCSEs, 'A' levels, Women's Studies, Languages, Basic Skills and some City and Guilds courses. Students, with guidance, compile a study plan suited to their own individual needs and goals when joining the programme. Their plan is revisited throughout the year during personal tutorials. Students may join at any point in the academic year and are offered the option of distance learning. They follow different learning pathways according to their level of confidence and skill. More than two thirds of students are women; most are white and from working-class backgrounds.

Access to Higher Education

The Access to Higher Education programme targets adults with no formal qualifications. It is validated by the Open College Network at Level Two and Level Three[2]. The programme is semi-modularised, with different combinations of subjects. Students may either follow a Science or 'Non-Science' pathway. The programme aims to be flexible and students may choose to study full or part time. About two thirds of the student body are women and most are white. There is a mixture of working-class and middle-class students, reflecting the local constituencies.

The programme aims to prepare students for higher education, and build self-confidence. Students are taught the dominant theories of the relevant academic field in anticipation of degree-level study. The radical discourses of the Access movement have not penetrated the programme at Ford College. For example, the terms 'social justice', 'social transformation' and 'student empowerment' are absent. The language of the market has become embedded in the Access programme. It was therefore important to provide opportunities for students to deconstruct the dominant discourses operating in the Access to HE programme. I had two chances to pursue this goal; first while I taught the Research Methods course on Access to HE for one term (Spring 1998/1999) and then in my role in curriculum development.

The Learning Pathway and Women's Studies

Over two years at Ford College, I created two new Open College Network[3] courses, expanding the Return to Study and Access to Higher Education programmes. My rationale for devising these courses was to:

1. expand opportunities for those excluded from education in the local community to take part in higher level study

2. encourage students to think critically

3. deconstruct dominant discourses with students

4. put class, ethnicity, gender, race and sexuality at the centre of analysis

5. develop collaborative pedagogies that address difference and remain committed to anti(hetero)sexist and antiracist practices.

The Learning Pathway offered Return to Study students a second year at Level Two or Three and was inspired by the Kennedy Report (Kennedy, 1997). It stimulated critical thinking and challenged hegemonic discourses.

I also organised a Women's Studies course. This was offered as an option to women on the Return to Study and Access to Higher Education courses. It provided an introduction to feminist theory and placed gender relations at the centre of analysis. The Women's Studies course enabled students to explore the connections between personal experience, knowledge and theory.

External moderation

While doing the research, I externally moderated a range of access courses at different colleges for a local Open College Network. As a moderator, I am responsible for externally verifying courses in terms of quality, standards, assessment, student satisfaction, recruitment and retention. I examine samples of student work to ensure that coursework and exams are set and assessed fairly and consistently and that feedback is clear, didactic and constructive. I confer with course tutors and meet with groups of students and I submit an annual report to the Open College Network. I always made entries in my research diary after moderation visits and kept a record of reports to refer to if needed in my research[4].

Policy contexts

My research coincided with burgeoning policy in the area of widening educational participation. The post-compulsory education sector is currently undergoing dramatic changes generated by such policy developments. Access education has been centralised by the appointment of the Quality Assurance Agency for Higher Education to oversee its operations, with a particular focus on standards. The discourse of 'widening educational participation' has overtaken, and to some extent replaced, discourses of 'Access' (Sand, 1998). Access to Higher Education courses have become increasingly vocationalised, instrumentally oriented and utilitarian, lacking an explicit political agenda (Barr, 1999). Such courses now represent a small part of the larger project for lifelong learning and widening educational participation.

This section describes and critiques the key policy texts emerging from the concern to widen educational participation.

Learning Works

Education must be at the heart of any inspired project for regeneration in Britain. It should be a springboard for the revitalisation that our communities so urgently need. However, in all the political debates, it is the economic rationale for increasing participation in education which has been paramount. Prosperity depends upon there being a vibrant economy, but an economy which regards its own success as the highest good is a dangerous one. Justice and equity must also have their claim upon the arguments for educational growth. In a social landscape where there is a growing gulf between those who have and those who have not, the importance of social cohesion cannot be ignored. (Kennedy, 1997:5-6)

The Widening Participation Committee was set up by the Further Education Funding Council (FEFC) in December 1994, chaired by Helena Kennedy QC. It set out to provide advice on promoting access to further education for those who 'do not participate in education and training, but who could benefit from it' (Kennedy, 1997:iii). The Committee's final report represented a powerful message about the importance of widening educational participation, not only for regenerating the national economy, but also on the moral and humanitarian principle of social equity and justice. The report revitalises the discourse characteristic of the early access movement, although it creates a 'shift from the terminology of 'access' to that of 'widening participation' (Sand, 1998:22).

The report argues that the competitive culture of the further education sector is a barrier to the promotion of access, and that providers need to collaborate rather than to compete through 'strategic partnerships' (Kennedy, 1997: 4). It also argues for the redistribution of public resources 'towards those with less success in earlier learning, moving towards equity of funding in post-16 education' (*ibid*.:13). Further recommendations include using lottery money to fund access initiatives, encouraging employers to invest in educational projects on behalf of their employees, reforming funding to address socio-economic deprivation directly and creating funding for childcare. The report advises a lifetime entitlement to education up to level 3 for all who are 'socially and economically deprived' and the creation of a 'new learning pathway', to provide 'a route through the wide range of opportunities in further education for adults' (Kennedy, 1996: 8).

The new learning pathway proposes innovative educational programmes that provide a combination of vocational, academic and critical education within a flexible framework that meets the diverse needs and backgrounds of adult students. Importantly, the new learning pathway concept recognises the valuable, alternative and highly creative contributions of many further education practitioners committed to widening educational participation. The report therefore publicly supports the non-conventional practices of access teachers, attempting to stretch such practices to all corners of the FE sector. Progressively, the report reclaims redistribution as a necessary strategy for educational inclusion and represents a 'passionate advocate for under-represented groups' (Sand, 1998:22).

The Learning Age

Following the Kennedy report, the government produced a Green Paper entitled *The Learning Age: a renaissance for a new Britain* (DfEE, February 1998). The paper fails to implement Kennedy's key proposals, taking no account of the endorsement of collaboration, raising entitlement to free education to level 3, redistribution of resources to the poorest sectors of society and the concept of new learning pathways.

The Learning Age emphasises the links between education and employment and the benefit of acquiring skills to 'increase earning power' (Sand, 1998:26). The central proposals are Individual Learning Accounts (ILAs) and the University for Industry (UfI). The ILAs, argues the Government, will encourage individual investment in learning, allowing people to 'take control of their learning'. Underpinning this proposal is the assertion that the responsibility for learning should be shared by the state, by individuals and by employers.

According to *The Learning Age*, the University for Industry will

> put the UK ahead of the rest of the world in using new technology to improve learning and skills... It will act as the hub of a brand new learning network, using modern communication technologies to link businesses and individuals to cost effective, accessible and flexible education and training. (DfEE, February 1998)

22

The DfEE produced a small booklet aimed at the general public outlining their proposals and promoting response through the small questionnaire attached (DfEE, February 1998). I ordered these booklets in bulk and disseminated them to students. I devoted one session with each student group to outlining *the Learning Age* and facilitating a feedback session. In small groups, students listed their views on flipchart paper, which they then shared with the rest of the class. Some of the students' points were:

- This is just another 'quick fix' to get people back into work.

- There will not be equal opportunity in education if people have to save up for their education – e.g. older people no longer working, families on low income.

- Employers may be reluctant to send employees for training because of the following:

  1. Will employees move to another job once trained?

  2. Who does their jobs while they're being trained?

(Access to HE students, 1998)

- Many people are scared of new technology and this is a huge barrier for mature people.

- Study at home will reinforce feelings of isolation. Learning in groups cannot be replaced – interaction, sharing and collaboration are very valuable to learning!

- The government should set up learning programmes in local schools and in the community for adults.

(Return to Study students, 1998)

A Return to Study student wrote the following in her student diary after our session on *The Learning Age*:

It is all very well for the Government to determine situations for us but what about the personal side of learning? We all learn from each other and we all make mistakes so how can learning through the Internet really teach us anything? We would become isolated and miss the individual attention that some of us require. We have tried for so long to train people for better prospects but now the idea

23

of the Individual Learning Accounts is to encourage employers to invest in people. This means that employers may lose their 'average' staff and be solely interested in upper management training. Examples of how difficult it is going to be for people are already apparent. Relating to class discussion, one student's husband couldn't decide which course to take on the Internet and while running up the phone bill realised that whatever he chose was going to cost him a minimum of £300. How can ordinary people afford this? Another example is a friend's husband that couldn't understand leaflets advertising information, so he gave in and didn't bother. All this boils down to bad guidance and teaching. The Government might want this country to be ahead in the learning and technology stakes but where does it leave our morals? Frankly I think it's all a lot of balderdash and much prefer the way I am learning. I need the group discussion, I need the related experiences and most of all I need the encouragement that my computer can't give me. (Vanessa, student diary, 29 April 1998)

The students' comments highlight the concerns of many adults when contemplating a return to education. These students deeply value the social aspects of learning. The human relationships that enrich their educational experiences cannot simply be replaced by computer technology. Against the discourse of the policy document, students' comments set guidance, tutor support and social interaction as crucial to effectively widening participation.

Learning to Succeed

Following the Green paper, the Government produced a white paper of 'its vision of the learning age', entitled *Learning to Succeed: a new framework for post-16 learning* (DfEE, June 1999). In this document, the concern to widen educational participation is explicitly connected to the government's welfare to work programmes (DfEE, June 1999:62). Policies initiated by the New Right, which block the unemployed and unpaid workers from accessing higher levels of education, remain in place and unchallenged:

Unemployed people and others not in employment can upgrade their skills through three main ways:

- Through access to further education without having to pay fees, and undertaking study of their own choice. *Those who are claiming Jobseekers Allowance (JSA) may not study, however, for more than 16 guided hours a week and they may remain subject to the availability for work conditions of JSA.* This is also the route available for those on New Deal for Lone Parents, New Deal for Partners of the Unemployed, and the New Deal for People with Disabilities;

- People on New Deal for 18-24 year olds and those over 25 have access to further education and training on a full-time basis on the advice of Personal Advisors *where this is thought the best way of overcoming barriers to re-entering the labour market.* This is paid for under contract from the Employment Service from New Deal funds; and

- Through TEC funded work based learning for adults, *which provides basic and occupational skills training for unemployed people* over the age of 25. (DfEE, June 1999: 62, emphasis added)

This policy makes participation on Access to Higher Education courses particularly difficult for those experiencing financial hardship.

Shelley: It's like if you want to do computers or basic reading, you can do that for nothing, but if you want to do something like counselling you've got to pay. Already it's streaming us, isn't it, into what we can be.

Kate: And really, basically, the government's programming us. (Women's Studies recorded group discussion, 1998)

Shelley and Kate recognise that there are particular areas of educational participation endorsed by policy and that these are at the lower levels of formal education. They are aware that opportunities are being constrained by the same policy that claims to be creating inclusion and equality. Policy emphasises basic skills, computer literacy and work-based skills. It makes no references to critical learning or higher education generally, unless this is individually financed.

The policy document enshrines the language of the market in the project to widen access. It shifts the discourse from access to *higher* education to access to *further* education. Indeed, Access to Higher Education courses are not once mentioned in the document, nor are the National Open College Network, despite the significant roles both have played in widening educational participation. Rather, NVQs (National Vocational Qualifications) are the focal point. The document proposes that the Qualification and Curriculum Authority, with National Training Organisations, will ensure that NVQs are 'based on standards which reflect the modern requirements of industry, while having a structure which allows more flexibility to better support the operations of individual firms' (DfEE, June 1999:48).

Neo-liberal discourse is privileged in the Learning Age, with key words and phrases being 'industry', 'business', 'employers', 'needs of local labour markets', 'customer needs', 'client groups' and 'independence'.

Political contexts

This section analyses the political contexts that have shaped the policy and practice of widening educational participation. Labour's 'third way' approach to widening participation is critiqued to highlight its dangers for marginalised groups.

The Third Way discourse

As the gap grows between the rich and the poor (Lothian Anti Poverty Alliance, 2001) and the world of work becomes increasingly characterised by de-regulation, casualisation, racialisation and feminisation (Thompson, 2000:1), anxieties are raised about individual and collective futures and stability. Lifelong learning has been constructed as a strategy to confront the economic challenges that face Britain. The Prime Minister claims that 'education is the best economic policy we have' (Ecclestone, 1999 cited in Thompson, 2000: 3).

This approach to education is rooted in the 'logic of neo-liberal globalisation' and the acceptance of the marketplace as the key to future stability (Jones, 1999: 238). Labour 'aims vigorously to police and regulate a system in which market forces now play a dynamic role' (*ibid.*).

Labour aims to create a 'culture of responsibility', an idea manifested in policy initiatives such as the New Deal. Education for literacy, key skills and citizenship is constructed as a strategy for economic competitiveness in the global market. Lifelong learning is seen as central to national stability. Through the normalising technologies of formal education, 'non-standard' students can be shaped into the 'good' citizens required for a strong British nation. Social exclusion is understood as a threat to the Nation, weakening the labour market and 'our' competitive position against the rest of the world.

Exploding policy of widening educational participation is part of the larger project to reform the Welfare State. The Prime Minister, proposing a 'third way', is intent on 'modernising' the welfare system to create a society of 'responsible citizens'. The Welfare State is perceived as being responsible for producing generations of dependent individuals who lack a work ethic. Giddens (The Prime Minister's intellectual advisor) describes a situation of 'moral hazard' whereby welfare provision has negatively altered people's behaviour, leading to their increased tendency to apply for assistance, avoid work for alleged health reasons and evade active job seeking (Giddens, 1998:115).

Giddens' analysis denies the legacy of institutionalised classism, colonialism, racism, and (hetero)sexism and ignores the root causes of poverty and unemployment in Britain. It conceals neo-colonialist discourses that reposition heterogeneous marginalised groups as a threat to 'British culture' and fails to make crucial links between poverty and the dominance of Western capitalism. It shifts the emphasis from social injustice and unequal power relations to 'failure' of traditional Labour policies and approaches, such as anti-racism. The rich critiques of the left are abandoned as ineffective and misguided, instead of developing new approaches, which address the complexity and diversity of social, economic and cultural inequity.

27

Overemphasis is placed on the ideal of individual responsibility; 'healthy' competition and independence, while values such as community relations and social justice are de-emphasised. The rhetorical device 'equality of worth' represents a move towards meritocracy, and the dismissal of all social policies which 'make the mistake' of giving 'something for nothing'. The Prime Minister envisages a society in which citizens 'rise according to their potential and talent, not privilege or class' (Blair quoted in White, 28 September 1999). A meritocratic model is adopted with the economic and social habits of a United States style free market. Individuals are expected to capitalise on policies such as the New Deal in order to improve their life chances. The government states clearly that a helping hand will only be given if the individual proves to be motivated to help themselves (Sherman, 1999). Social problems are individualised, so constructing antiracist and anti-sexist approaches as romantic and idealistic but unrealistic, misguided and even damaging.

The market is seen as the solution to the 'culture of dependence'. The goal is to minimise the role of the State in the arena of education, health and social security, while slowly weaning individuals off their 'dependence' on the 'free ride' provided by welfare provision. Education and the National Health Service will slowly be replaced or supplemented by private enterprise, with experts in business moving in to solve the inadequacies of a publicly run education and health sector (Carvel, 1999).

Giddens interprets equality as inclusion and inequality as exclusion (Giddens, 1998: 102). Inclusion he sees as synonymous with citizenship, the civil and political rights and responsibilities of all members of society. In his definition, he includes opportunities and involvement in 'public space', and claims work and education to be two main contexts of opportunity (*ibid.*: 103). His analysis of social exclusion as a dual process is insightful. He identifies two forms of exclusion, those at the bottom, cut off from mainstream opportunities, and 'voluntary exclusion', the withdrawal of affluent groups from public institutions (*ibid.*). He recognises the interdependence of the dual processes of exclusion and the significance of combating *voluntary exclusion* for creating an inclusive society.

However, his thinking takes no account of the interdependence of the poverty cycle and the wealth cycle (Young, 1999: 213). Policy targets exclusion at the bottom and fails to tackle voluntary exclusion. Small amounts of additional resources have been made available through initiatives such as Education Action Zones, but these depend too heavily on local voluntary business support and self-help (*ibid.*). Power and Whitty point out that some of the zone initiatives are based on 'a deficit model of local communities and 'problem' parents and children', having the potential 'to pathologize rather than to empower, to exclude rather than to include' (1999: 544). With a rhetorical emphasis on 'equality of worth', Labour revitalises the ideal of meritocracy as the key to social inclusion and equality of opportunity.

As Professor Taylor-Goobi states:

> Government policies emphasise opportunities. Labour says those who fail to take those opportunities and make their own provisions are punished, by losing benefits. But this hits those who come from the poorest backgrounds the hardest. (Taylor-Gooby, 1999)

Greg's words illustrate the despair connected to limited opportunities:

> *I used to think – I'm just useless at this and I'm just useless at that – but the reason was...I didn't want to be a decorator, I didn't want to be on building sites, that was the reason, not because I was useless.* (Greg, Return to Study recorded group discussion, 1998)

The concept of meritocracy clearly poses problems for marginalised groups. The third way discourse is embedded in a colonial, neo-colonial and racist ideology. For example, in our colonial past, the white man set out to 'civilise' the natives in the name of 'progress' and assimilation into a 'superior' culture. The discourse of widening educational participation, particularly as articulated by Labour, assumes paternalistic, racist and classist postures of drawing 'the excluded' into the superior 'enterprise culture' and 'risk society'.

Giddens (1998) proposes the replacement of the welfare state with 'the social investment state'. The role of the state will be to encourage individuals to take risks rather than provide social security. Yet Professor Taylor-Gooby (1999) concludes from statistics that 'risk society is an individualist idea which fails to see there are entire groups with difficulties in finding and keeping work' (*ibid.*).

Third way politics emphasises competition and the generation of wealth (Giddens, 1998: 99). The State's primary role is to develop an entrepreneurial culture and a 'society of risk takers' (*ibid.*: 100), prioritising the 'cultivation of human potential' (*ibid.*: 101). The Welfare State is seen as undemocratic, because it 'depends on top-down distribution of benefits' and fails to provide the 'space for civil liberty' (*ibid.*: 112-113). The focus has shifted from the concern with human emancipation to an interest in emancipating human skill and talent.

> And all around us is the challenge of change. The challenge is how? The answer is people. The future is people. The liberation of human potential not just as workers but as citizens. People are born with talent and everywhere it is in chains. Fail to develop the talents of any one person, we fail Britain. Talent is 21st-century wealth. Every person liberated to fulfil their potential adds to our wealth. (Tony Blair quoted in *The Times*, 29 September 1999)

British citizens are constructed as resources for the nation's competitive position in the global market. They are seen as citizens with rights and responsibilities primarily as waged workers, implying a specific model of work.

The industrial-patriarchal concept of work

Mechthild Hart's conceptualisation of the industrial-patriarchal model of work (Hart, 1992) reveals how current policy exacerbates the vulnerability of marginalised groups in British society. She explains that we cannot discuss education without

> ...taking notice of the current dramatic shifts and changes affecting the organisation and distribution of work, and the nature and actual content of work and work-related skills, knowledge and experiences. (Hart, 1992:1)

The main priority of industry is to find the cheapest labour possible (*ibid.*; see also Holland with Frank and Cooke, 1998; Aronowitz and Di Fazio, 1994; Reich, 1992) and globalisation and technology has made this increasingly easy. Because of capital mobility[5], employers have an effective mechanism to keep wages low.

Giddens also marks out globalisation as a key characteristic of contemporary society, but he claims that this is not an issue about social justice (Giddens, 1998: 67). Further issues that, he contends, fall outside of emancipatory politics include scientific and technological change and our relationship to the natural world (*ibid.*). Hart's analysis boldly exposes the reasons why Gidden's claims are dangerous for vulnerable groups within and without British society.

She borrows the concept of the 'housewifization of labour'[6] to reveal the 'systematic utilisation of the sexual division of labour to cheapen both male and female labour' (Hart, 1992: 20). Her analysis focuses on work relations rather than specific tasks and kinds of labour. The housewife is regarded as a structural category revealing the 'organising principle of the (capitalist) sexist division of labour' behind both male and female labour (*ibid.*: 21).

Hart compares 'normal' wage labour to 'marginal' wage labour, noting the increasing numbers of workers in marginal labour across the globe (see also Pearson, 2000). The conditions of marginal labour are similar to housework; no legal protection, no benefits, sickness pay or holidays, often precarious and very poorly paid. The conditions are further characterised by there being no hope of promotion, being tied to the means of production and linked to forms of direct and indirect coercion (*ibid.*: 23). 'Marginal' labour is to 'normal' labour what the housewife is to the male breadwinner.

Comparison illustrates the implications of a shift from social security to risk. The already wide divisions between rich and poor, secure and insecure, deepen, with the poorest groups being 'encouraged' to take risks. For example, lone parents are now 'encouraged' to leave the security of benefits to retrain for work. Many are bound to end up in marginal work.

The discourses of security and risk position subjects differently in relation to family, work and education. Security signifies a negative concept of (feminised and racialised) dependence while risk represents (masculinist and white-raced) independence. For example, Hilda explains that her decision to quit college to find paid work is connected to the break-up of her marriage and her refusal to 'be on income support and be a single parent'.

> I think when I first came to College I was very determined that I'd have a new career by the end of it, and I felt, after the first year, that I was capable of doing that, and so I went on to the Access course, hoping to go on to do a degree. But now, I'm umm, I've come to the point now that I don't think its going to lead me to that unfortunately because I'm now separated and I need to get back to work and I'll have to go back to what I was doing before. So from that point of view it's very disappointing. If I could afford it I would study full-time. Now that we're separated and I'm not getting any income from my husband, I feel I need to get some money coming in and get back into the real world. I could study, stay on income support and be a single parent, but I don't want to do that. (Hilda, 1999)

Hilda sees herself as a single parent *only when claiming welfare benefits*, but perceives herself as 'part of the real world' when she is in paid work.

Women's Work and the Market

> In a market society where social value is directly measured in monetary equivalents, anything that is 'naturally' available and therefore can be appropriated free of cost is essentially worthless. (Hart, 1992: 26)

Naturalising mothering and housework renders the exploitation of women's labour legitimate (*ibid.*: 24).

> The housewife whose work is (ideally) entirely free of charge, must inevitably become the ideal form of labour, representing the highest degree of cheapness. (*ibid.*: 26)

Women are often constructed as *naturally* capable of work that involves attention to detail, flexibility, patience, care and repetition – the kinds of skills required in housework. Within the current labour market, such skills are sought after. Consequently, women are entering paid work in greater numbers than men, and this is often seen as proof of their increasing social power. Yet their participation in paid work is clearly linked to sexist stereotypes. As more men experience unemployment, women find themselves in situations where family survival depends on their accepting poorly paid, marginal work (*ibid*.: 37). Indeed, such conditions of Black women's work experiences in Britain were powerfully documented over fifteen years ago (Bryan, Dadzie and Scafe, 1985).

Hart identifies problematic links between lifelong learning and work. Colleges are expected to prepare their 'customers' for the world of work through the acquisition of Key and Basic Skills. Basic Skills includes reading, writing, mathematics and communication. Key Skills include computing, team co-operation, interpersonal skills, problem solving and 'flexibility'. These skills prepare individuals for the expanding service industry, where they will be expected to project a 'positive image' on behalf of their employer. Key skills also emphasise 'coping' in stressful situations, teaching students to control 'negative' emotions such as anger (one of the units on the Return to Study course includes *Negative and Positive Emotions*). The immediate benefit of developing coping skills in an increasingly stressful world is certainly clear. Yet ultimately it serves the interests of the employer, providing a mechanism of social control and manipulating workers into accepting the individual responsibility to cope in inhumane and exploitative situations. Potential workers are formally taught the 'value' of coping by repressing 'negative' feelings of anger when they have been treated unjustly (Hart, 1992). The following extract highlights the way such strategies operate to lead students to believe anger represents 'weakness':

> *One of my weaknesses is to address people in a rather harsh manner when I feel strongly about something they have done or I believe in. I know I have to learn to control this abrupt manner and I am aware of it more than ever now. My reason for being this way is because I am a bit of a crusader. If I can fight for rights that will help others then I will do so.* (Vanessa, Personal Statement, October 1997)

Discouraged from critical awareness, students are taught to cope with 'stressful' situations which are seen as a natural part of everyday life. According to this logic, the individual who cannot cope is 'unsuccessful'. The problem resides in the 'flawed' *individual*. Thus are the *social* aspects of poverty, exploitation and social exclusion concealed.

The neo-liberal discourse of widening participation constructs access education as a project to enable disadvantaged individuals to improve their basic skills for work (Dawe, 1999; Stuart, 1999), producing individuals with 'higher skills'. The discourse silences important issues such as the diminishing of jobs in Britain due to the efficiency of computerised technology and the drive for cheap labour. As employers manufacture products wherever labour is cheapest, employees are increasingly powerless to negotiate better pay and conditions, whether or not they have 'higher skills'. Indeed, it is becoming apparent that a university degree no longer guarantees employment or a salary above poverty level. A study conducted by the Higher Education Funding Council for England reveals that this situation is racialised and gendered. Their research showed that graduates from ethnic minority backgrounds are up to three times more likely than their white counterparts to end up unemployed (Major, 16 May 2000). Their findings also pointed to the importance of the body. In general, tall men benefit from higher earnings while obese women are paid less than other employees (*ibid.*). These findings have been unpublished due to worries lest exposure to these realities undermine policy initiatives:

> Given the government's policy to widen access, it would be perverse to produce an indicator that would have the effect of discouraging institutions from recruiting such students. (HEFC quoted in *ibid.*)

These factors, combined with increasing levels of competition, cause various levels of insecurity and vulnerability for all paid workers, including those in the new professions. For example, further education lecturers are experiencing the conditions of marginal labour, with temporary and part-time positions. As the FE sector is restructured, they are expected to demonstrate flexibility in their work. Always in jeopardy of losing their jobs, tutors must successfully recruit and retain large numbers of students, juggle piles of administrative work, be available to support students whenever necessary, cope with increasing levels of bureaucracy, ensure their students achieve and progress – all while being paid for a shorter week (Sellers, 1998). The juggling act expected of tutors is also expected of mature students.

Mature students can juggle lots of things

In March 1999, Tessa Blackstone (minister for education) led a national relaunch of Access to Higher Education. In her keynote address, she made clear her commitment to widening access and the government's acknowledgement of the success of Access to HE courses. She also applauded the success of mature students to juggle study with maintaining other commitments in their lives.

In 1997, the government decided to radically reform the student funding system by replacing grants with loans and introducing tuition fees. This has significantly affected the undergraduate student population (Major, October 1998). Mature students from poorer socio-economic backgrounds must calculate the risk of debt and negotiate complex funding systems before accessing education. Consequently, Access to Higher Education co-ordinators have sadly witnessed student numbers dropping year by year across Britain (Wicks, 2000; Sand *et al*, 1999). It is astonishing that there is any surprise, as the entry of mature, ethnic minority, female and working class students into higher education thins out dramatically after such fundamental changes in student funding occurred.

In her speech, Blackstone implicitly responded to these circumstances, by referring to the proven success of mature students to juggle study, work and family. Her argument was that mature students who deserve educational opportunities are capable of supporting themselves through part-time study. She thus excludes individuals who are unable to cope with multiple responsibilities at once.

The following comment demonstrates the problem with pressuring mature students to perform juggling acts:

> *I was so enthusiastic and so keen to do well and I worked so hard that um I ended up getting burn-out and I collapsed. And uh, I was just sort of completely exhausted, 'cause I was working at night to do, to pay for the course as well. Because I was doing the course part-time, I didn't get a grant or anything, so I was looking after the children during the day, working in a casualty emergency department of the hospital at night and then at university two or three days a week. So I was total burn-out, I was very very poorly.*
> (Charity, 1999)

Placing emphasis on coping ability implicitly justifies the removal of key support systems such as grants and this has significant implications for widening access. There is a clear contradiction between new student funding arrangements and the concern to widen educational access.

Accessing education in context

The discourse of widening educational participation needs to be collaboratively deconstructed in order to mobilise radical discourses in the interests of access students. The dominant discourse places access students in precarious and vulnerable situations in relation to globalisation, technological change and the creation of a society of risk-takers. It prioritises the national economy and individualised 'success' as the guiding purpose for widening participation. It therefore enshrines particular ways of understanding the world. Through the hegemonic discourse of widening educational participation, a Western, masculinist, middle-class and white cultural perspective, is reprivileged.

Access education needs to be collaboratively refashioned to address issues of social injustice. Access students simultaneously require a strategy of redistribution of funds (as suggested by Kennedy, 1997) and the recognition of their specific, although heterogeneous, needs and experiences. Such a project requires the collaboration of practitioners, students and academics. This book represents such a project, which is why collaboration with students is central. In the next chapter I consider the importance of collaborative approaches to researching access education.

Notes

1   All names of places and people have been changed to maintain anonymity.

2   Level Three is described by NOCN as 'the acquisition of a more complex range of competences, knowledge and understanding in contexts which develop autonomous, analytical and critical abilities that prepare the learner to progress to further independent achievements' (NOCN, 2000).

3   The Learning Pathway was developed in collaboration with the Return to Study staff team, who contributed ideas about its content and organisation. The Women's Studies course was inspired by a course that I externally moderate. I asked the programme creator/organiser how she would feel if I used her course as a basis to set up a similar course at Ford College. She was delighted by the idea, expressing that this signified for her what feminism was about: the sharing of knowledge to expand ideas that contribute to the general goals of feminism.

4   I sought permission from course tutors and students before collecting and using this data for my research.

5   Capital mobility is the ability to ship raw materials to the developing world for assembly and then export it back.

6   This term was coined by a group of West German sociologists at the Bielefeld Centre for Sociology of Development. See Mies, 1986.

3
Towards a Methodology of Collaboration

> ...the role of an educational researcher is always to work in specific circumstances *with* rather than on or even for the people who inhabit them... Such a way of working is also a way of dealing with some of the arrogance presupposed in some forms of knowledge, and their implication in structures of dominance and oppression. (Griffiths, 1998: 111)

This chapter describes the process of developing collaborative, interactive and reflexive methodological approaches. It challenges accounts of social research that trace a linear and progressive path from start to finish

Reflexive collaboration

My aim to develop collaborative research approaches was inspired by feminist methodology concerned with empowering and non-exploitative research (Ribbens and Edwards, 1998; Maynard and Purvis, 1994) and with poststructuralist critiques of positivism (Usher, 1997; Lather, 1991). Lather describes a 'postpositivist era' characterised by 'an increased visibility for research designs that are interactive, contextualized, and humanly compelling because they invite joint participation in exploration of research issues' (Lather, 1991: 52).

I am committed to joint participation, and researching my own students provided opportunities for such interaction. This helped to identify important interconnections between the private (e.g. their experiences of family and mothering, the emotional and subjective) and the public (e.g. their experiences of access education) as lived out by the women and men participating in the research. Such interconnections have crucial ramifications for understanding, deconstructing and reshaping meanings around adult educational participation. The collaborative approach enabled students to contribute actively to a research project of which they felt they had some ownership. Reflexivity was central to the research, which acknowledged the 'world-making', 'constructive quality of research' (Usher, 1997: 36).

> It is in a sense to *research* the research, to bend the research back on itself, to ask by what practices, strategies and devices is worldmaking achieved? By asking this question, the research act is made self-referential or *reflexive*. (*ibid*. original emphasis)

Reflexivity in teaching and research requires an examination of how our values affect our work in the classroom and in the field (Lather, 1991:80). Reflexive researchers reject universalised claims to knowledge and challenge theory that forbids knowledge emerging from the personal, subjective and emotional (Ellsworth, 1992). Values, culture, and social positioning are not dynamics that can be removed or isolated whenever it is convenient. Rather, all the participants are entrenched in the historical, geographical, political, personal, economic, psychological and social dynamics of the moment, shaping their interpretations, perceptions and ways of knowing (Ellsworth, 1997; Flax, 1995; Kenway, 1995; Luke and Gore, 1992). Such understandings of research processes and relations were crucial to the production of this ethnography of widening educational participation.

Constructing a feminist post-structural ethnography

Ethnography engages with the lives of those being studied and attempts to 'fully acknowledge and utilise subjective experience as an intrinsic part of the research' (Davies, 1999:4-5). It contributed strongly to the creation of collaboration between co-participants. My intense involvement in the world of access education, as a student, teacher, researcher and external examiner, enabled me to participate in the research at a variety of levels. I used such multi-level involvement as a resource for collaboration. Knowing that I too was a mature student enhanced the relationship of trust with students, encouraging interaction that included me as a co-participant of the research. Students identified with me as a mature student with children who experienced many of the same daily frustrations and hurdles as they did. Like me, they understood motherhood as connected to every aspect of their lives, as hugely influential in the ways they made sense of the world and as a valuable experience in the reconstruction of theory. Equally, I identified with them, and this interpersonal dynamic of 'sameness' (Hey, 2000: 176) enhanced the production of ethnography, and especially of collaboration.

The experiences of the co-participants provide a resource for understanding the discourses of access education and widening participation. How do these discourses affect the lives of students negotiating access provision? What do the autobiographies of access students reveal about dominant discourses of widening educational participation? What impact does educational participation have on the lives, relationships and subjectivities of access students? How is subjectivity reproduced through the discursive field of access education?

Feminist poststructural perspectives of 'experience' have illuminated the theoretical limitations and simplifications entangled in unproblematic notions of experience.

> While language in the form of different competing discourses does indeed give meaning to events retrospectively, this meaning is not the reflection of an already fixed reality but a version of meaning. (Weedon, 1997:78)

The crucial point is that this 'version of meaning' is significant. It provides a resource for deconstructing how we make sense of our experiences within specific social contexts. By understanding the narration of an experience as one *version* of it and not the *un-*

covering of a fixed reality, we can imagine and create change. So, when a mature student comes to the classroom believing that her school experience is evidence of an intrinsic lack of academic ability, a deconstruction of her experience may lead to a new under-standing that repositions her as a knowing subject.

Although I work with a concept of experience as problematic, ack-nowledging that it is constituted by discourse and is diverse, multiple, contradictory, complex and socially constructed, I accept that 'experience' is a valuable resource:

> The feminist case that where social relations of gender are sub-ordinating, then they should be transformed, rests on accounts of the experiences of the subordinated/subordinating, as well as the theory of subordination. The judgement of what should be changed is clearly political and ethical. To identify what should be trans-formed, we need appropriate theory: to produce appropriate theory we need knowledge of what is to be transformed, and so some sense of how subordination is experienced. (Ramazanoglu and Holland, 1999: 383)

I also see *research relationships* as crucial for producing ethno-graphy. The research process involves forming and maintaining close relationships built on trust and reciprocity and this inescapably and rightly involves the emotional:

> The contrived context of initial, and sometimes long-term, relations must be set alongside the reality of feelings, emotions, lasting friendship and occasionally painful memories that they can bring. Both parties in field relationships can find these 'work' relations meaningful, reciprocal and based on shared commitment. (Coffey, 1999: 55)

This under-theorised but rich and relevant aspect of doing ethno-graphy needs to be explored and written into the ethnographic text. The relationship I formed with my participants was hugely reward-ing, supportive and validating. Occupying the dual positions of teacher and researcher created intensity in the research process. Often my role as a teacher had no professional cut-off points, caus-ing tensions between my personal and professional life. Students telephoned me in the late evenings and early mornings, came over for coffee and had long chats with me in the school playground or at the supermarket, a source of irritation to my family, who had to cope with the intense level of my work relationships. The ethnographic nature of the research reinforced and complicated the interconnections between the private, personal and public realms of my life. The relationships developed through sameness and difference were crucial to the production of knowledge through the research process.

The research participants

The 23 participants were access students at Ford College. Thirteen students were on the Return to Study programme, three on the Access to Higher Education programme and seven moved from Return to Study to Access. I taught Return to Study, Women's Studies, Qualitative Research Methods and GCSE Sociology. All participants were taught by me as well as by other tutors in the College. This complexity of relationships provided rich data but it also generated ethical dilemmas.

Asking my students to participate in the research raised ethical issues but they generally appeared to feel positive about it, especially as their experiences were being valued and legitimised through the research process. For mature 'non-traditional' students, low self-esteem and low confidence are common after years of being positioned as 'non-academic' or 'low-achievers'. Women, in particular, are often positioned as 'low-level achievers' according to dominant discourses about 'success' that validate specific kinds of achievement. Achievements located in the world of academia, politics, industry and business are publicly recognised. Achievement in the domestic realm, raising a family for example, is represented as a natural phenomenon and disassociated from success and skill (Hanmer, 1997; Jackson, 1997; Nicolson, 1997). Involvement in research that focused on their lives affirmed that their experiences were important. Beverly Skeggs, who also researched her students, explains:

> Many of the young women conf irmed Ann Oakley's observations
> that they could not believe they were interesting enough to be any

use to a study. The students' sense of self-worth was enhanced by being given an opportunity to be valued, knowledgeable and interesting. In the follow-up studies this continues to be important. This challenges the idea that the researched are just objects of a voyeuristic bourgeois gaze. (Skeggs, 1994: 81)

Feeling vulnerable: issues of power

The aim to conduct non-exploitative, empowering research has led many feminists to favour qualitative methods (Ribbens and Edwards, 1998; Stanley, 1992; Oakley, 1990). Others have challenged the common sense link between feminist methodology and qualitative methods. The level of intimacy generated through qualitative research has been noted as both empowering and exploitative (Skeggs, 1995b; Kelly, Burton and Regan, 1994) and it was important to explore in my research.

I tried to maintain a reciprocal relationship with participants by sharing personal stories with them but this was not enough to balance out the power relations. There were moments that I felt vulnerable as I stepped outside of the boundaries set through dominant discourses of professionalism. I was committed to working in ways that challenged the rules of convention, yet I often felt vulnerable about my job and my success as a doctoral student because of my oppositional approaches.

Similarly, students often expressed their anxieties and feelings of vulnerability about disclosing to me their intimate thoughts and experiences. It was risky to expose their frustrations and dissatisfactions about their access courses and tutors. After all, their tutors were positioned to determine their academic success or failure. So I had to be very careful about how I used or discarded certain of the pieces of information I collected.

My role as a colleague *and* as a researcher raised further ethical dilemmas. Although my colleagues initially agreed to the research, I sensed that it sometimes made them uncomfortable. One of them worried lest I interview her students after a class when she was having an 'off-day' and they represent her in a negative light. The research was certainly not about undermining the work of my peers, but I had to be very sensitive about using or discarding interesting data, in light of the students' and colleagues' feelings of insecurity.

Ultimately I decided to include data that contributed significantly to the project. The best I could do to resolve the dilemma between the interests of individual subjects and the aims of the project, was to maintain the anonymity and confidentiality of the study by changing the names of people, places and courses. The contradictions between feminist politics, goals of empowerment, collaboration, inclusion of significant data and exclusion of 'sensitive' data, cannot be fully resolved. These competing concerns raise serious dilemmas for the researcher but being reflexive is paramount.

Although my dual position as teacher and researcher generated these ethical dilemmas, it also opened up exciting possibilities for innovative and collaborative research.

Developing collaborative research approaches
The concern to develop collaborative approaches positioned students with me as 'co-participants'. This enabled:

- different educational experiences (teaching and learning) and the interconnections between experience, power and positionality to be examined
- the discourses of widening participation to be collaboratively deconstructed and reshaped
- methods, methodology and pedagogy to be developed with participants
- approaches to data analysis to be interactive.

The project was underpinned by the principle that theory must be grounded in practice, and this led to experimenting with theory in the classroom. Writing a book based on what I read and what people said in interviews was an extremely limited way to develop strategies for widening participation. The co-participants needed to live out the theories within the particular context of the classroom and think through this experience together.

The opportunity to put these ideas into practice emerged when I was teaching Qualitative Research Methods for the first time. We had a lively discussion about how research contributes to and challenges unequal power relations. Although I came to the lesson with a course outline, the students decided to drop the formal agenda and explore research through discussing our shifting questions and ideas. They suggested that we use my PhD research as focus point.

This classroom experiment significantly shaped my research and also our understanding of research processes and relations. It enabled us to conduct a collaborative examination of key themes emerging from the participants' accounts and from theory and, in turn, helped identify important links between methodological and pedagogical issues. For example, my concern to put critical pedagogical theory into practice resonated with their frustration with conventional 'banking-type' approaches to teaching and learning (Freire, 1972). We looked at ways that research could transform pedagogical approaches which centred on students' contributions and insights. How could this collaborative project contribute to the development of strategies for widening participation that centred on students' needs, interests and experiences?

Our discussions focused on questions of power relations and epistemology. Whose knowledge is privileged in educational research and within access classrooms? We applied these questions to general and specific contexts, raising more questions. How could we disrupt the re-privileging of certain sets of knowledge, while others were discounted and silenced? How could we retain a politics of difference, where diverse and conflicting voices were validated and respected? How could we simultaneously maintain a commitment to anti-classist, antiracist and anti(hetero)sexist practices?

The students contributed to these complex ideas and questions, and really pushed my own thinking. I felt extremely grateful for this experience. They kept saying that their thinking had never been stretched like this before. It was a special and exciting term.

Our approach also raised problems of methodological significance. It was I who brought the idea of collaboration to the classroom. It is difficult to assess whether the participants really experienced the course and the research as collaborative. Most likely their experience was varied and shifting in relation to positionality, power dynamics, and their own confidence-level and access to analytical tools. It is possible that the experiment sometimes reinforced exclusions. Yet there were crucial moments when participants were empowered. The collaborative approaches enabled temporary but significant moments of destabilising unequal power relations to occur in the field and the access classroom.

Certain complex issues contributed to the opportunity to experiment in the course. First, I was assigned, on short notice, to teach the course for one term, because I was the only staff member experienced in and practising qualitative research. The absence of formal assessment criteria for the course allowed a freedom not usually enjoyed in further education. It is significant that I did not enter the course with any strategy for experimental collaboration but that it was the group of students as much as my current thinking that led us to create this experimental course together. Indeed, I felt that one student in particular, John, encouraged the collaborative approach. John had a developed interest in issues of social change, power and inequality and the other students admired his contributions and were inspired by his ideas. The relationships between the co-participants created a unique platform for experimental and collaborative approaches but sometimes exacerbated power inequalities in the classroom:

> Helen said she felt that without any structure at all it made it very difficult for those who were less confident to speak out loud in class – she felt that sometimes I was – and John was – 'too deep'. She explained that sometimes this was intimidating and confusing for the rest of the group. John reacted by saying 'I knew I should have just shut up' and the group immediately reassured him that they wanted him to speak and were very interested in what he had to say. I asked them whether they now regretted the 'experiment' and would have preferred to continue from plan one when I started to give a lecture on positivism. The answer from the group was a firm 'NO!' and Lisa said 'we've come too far!' (Research Diary, 9 February 1999)

Despite the reflexivity exercised by the group, power imbalances did not disappear. But they became more visible and easier to speak about. We developed an ethos where students supported one another, critically examined relationships and used such lived examples as resources for thinking through the research design for my PhD.

Collaborative methods

This section sets out the tools of data collection developed collaboratively through discussions among the participants.

Interactive discussions

We replaced interviews with 'interactive conversations', a method that aims to generate reflexive and non-exploitative research (Appleby, 1994). In conventional social research, the strategy of silence is upheld as essential in interviewing (Fielding,1993: 150-151). Feminist, antiracist, post-colonial and post-structuralist theorists (Paulston, 2000; Usher, 1997; Stanley and Wise, 1993; Lather, 1991; Harding, 1991; Bertaux, 1981) have highlighted the problems embedded in this approach. Appleby argues:

> Silence in interviews appears to follow non-interactive and non-directive models which conveys powerful messages... Not only is the passage of information one way, as in the traditional interview model, but also disclosure is one way: from the interviewee to the interviewer. The interviewee and their unconsciousness become objectified as the object/s of data. (Appleby, 1994: 6)

As their tutor, my relationship with the participants was built on trust, support, discussions and friendship, which made it impossible to remain unresponsive to their spoken narratives. To stay quiet while they shared with me their pain, joy, hopes, fears and feelings of failure and success, would suggest that I did not really care about their lives. But I did care about their lives, and they were familiar with my perspectives through our work in the classroom.

We decided that conversations and discussions were the way forward for our project. My research diary traces the evolution of this strategy, for example:

In today's Qualitative Research Methods lesson, we decided that in terms of group discussions, some format of open questions was needed. After some consideration, we finally decided that we would each contribute questions, which we would bring in two weeks, and then collectively select questions for our group discussion. (Research diary, 23 February 1999)

When we met two weeks later, the students had forgotten their list of questions. At first I felt disappointed but, upon reflection, this signalled several important issues. The project ultimately was mine, not theirs, and I had far more to gain from it (a doctoral degree) than they did. Although the participants were keen to collaborate during their scheduled lessons, it was an imposition to expect them to invest personal time. Outside of the classroom, they were engrossed in other areas of their lives that demanded their time and attention. My relationship to the project was different because my PhD was much more important in *my* life than in *theirs*. Different levels of investment and benefit inevitably limited their collaboration.

Autobiography as method

Feminist accounts of autobiography captured my attention (Birch, 1998: 175; Mauthner, 1998b: 46-49; Stanley, 1993). Autobiography as method is used 'to place subjectivity, emotions, memory and analysis of experience, and the link between individual experience and social, political and familial processes', at the centre of knowledge production (Mauthner, 1998b: 47).

Autobiography as method also evolved out of collaboration with participants. After examining my research proposal, we carefully considered using different methods. We thought about the construction of narratives in research and decided that the written autobiography may create an empowering space for participants to represent their life stories. Participants would to some extent be in control of how, what and when they wrote. I suggested that I could read through their stories in advance of our interactive conversations, so that we could then discuss the issues raised in their autobiographies.

In practice, this did not happen. Again, the participants were busy with their own courses and personal lives and most were unable to write an autobiography before the interactive conversation. Some became anxious about writing an autobiography and requested further clarification. So although we hoped they would all feel in control of how and what they wrote, I ended up providing guidelines. I finally received autobiographies of various lengths and styles, ranging from two to eleven pages. These reflected the interaction between my guidance, their memory work, and the craft of carefully constructing a piece of writing intended for another person, in this case their tutor.

Diaries and the autobiographical

Over a period of three years (1997-2000), I kept a research diary of my experiences of teaching at the College. I recorded my observations of classroom relations, and mapped out my journey as a teacher trying to challenge unequal power relations in the adult education department. I was interested in the emotional structuring of these relations. The research diary created a thinking space for me to write and reflect through the resistances, challenges and problems that arose. This intimately connected data collection (keeping a research diary), data analysis (reflecting on my diary), with the act of writing (which generated thought and analysis) as overlapping stages.

Inevitably, my research diary represents no more than a partial account. As Bell points out, the research diary is 'directed to an audience outside the text' (Stanley, 1993: 48), relating personal to wider public meanings' and is therefore incomplete (Bell, 1997: 82). I selected the diary entries to include in this book, according to the public nature of producing a book as well as to their relevance.

The student diaries were also useful both pedagogically and methodologically. I encouraged students to use diaries as a reflexive approach to learning, to reflect on their learning, to develop social and self-awareness and critically to evaluate their experiences of learning more systematically.

As a research tool:

> each diary entry – unlike life histories – is sedimented into a particular moment in time: they do not emerge 'all at once' as reflections on the past, but day by day strive to record an ever-changing present. (Plummer, 1990: 17–18 in Bell, 1997: 73)

Diaries offered insight into the ever-changing experiences of being an adult student. The participants made immediate records of how they felt about different aspects of learning. As with written autobiographies, the students constructed their diary entries with me in mind, their imaginary and real audience, and this shaped their writing so that their personal reflection was designed for the public realm of educational research. The power dynamics and identity formations inherent in these processes required scrutinising when the data was analysed.

Data analysis

Data analysis poses specific problems for collaborative research with regard to its selective and interpretative aspects. As the researcher selects, interprets and represents the data, the intended meanings of the participants inevitably become distorted and reshaped. Data analysis is generally an isolated process, which slices participants' narratives into pieces of text coded by themes and consistencies.

In conventional accounts, data analysis is presented as the stage following fieldwork and before writing-up. This differs from my experience of the research process, which was characterised by 'sequential analysis' (Becker, 1971). Analysis was on-going and overlapping, extending before, over and beyond the life of the project. My analytical engagement with access education began as an Access to Higher Education student, as I identified it as the focus for my PhD, and continued through the fieldwork, literature review, transcribing, rereading, discussing and writing about the data. I discussed emerging themes with the students, using the space of the classroom as a critical arena for analysis. We talked about their decisions to return to study, their understandings of learning and education, teaching and classroom dynamics, intimidation, exclusions, changes, choices and identity. This active and interactive process led to our reformulating research questions and enabled co-participants to reflect on the perspectives, interpretations, theories and the knowledge generated through this process.

The friendships we developed enriched our collaborative approaches to data analysis. During casual chats with them, I often checked out my thinking about certain data.

> *Kerry asked me if our recorded meeting was of help and I explained to her just how helpful it was. I summarised my analysis of her comments and experiences, and she agreed with my interpretation saying 'exactly, exactly!' We spoke about how her knowledge and experiences were just as valuable as anyone else's and she said that she now knows this to be true. I thanked her for her contribution and she said 'I am so glad I could help you and you can chat to me any time for help, because you have helped me through so much'.*
> (Research diary, 2 December 1999)

The participants appeared relaxed while they discussed the data with me in informal meetings. This often led me to rethink and modify the analysis, forming a strategy for developing interactive analysis that had a significant effect on the final textual version of the research.

Dilemmas in collaborative analysis

I wanted the research to go through a process of collaborative analysis. This raised particular dilemmas, for example, the issue of differential 'access to discursive resources' (Skeggs, 1995b: 201). Initially, I envisaged facilitating critical discussions about sections of my written analysis. However, this may have generated intimidation and anxiety, as following what I had written required an understanding of certain theories. I had to write the text in an accessible way, so that students and practitioners could engage with it.

> *Today Dorothy came over for a chat. I shared Chapter Seven with her, particularly because I wanted her feedback about how I analysed her accounts. After she read through parts of the Chapter, she expressed her agreement with my analysis and also com-*

mented that she was surprised by how easy it was to read. She explained that she expected it to be 'really academic' and therefore impossible to understand. (Research Diary, October 2000)

However, the contradictory imperatives of writing accessibly for participants and writing for the academy reveal some of the ambiguities and contradictions feminist poststructural researchers face. Patricia Hills Collins (2001) has also highlighted the exclusivity of much poststructural language. I think this is a particular problem that needs to be addressed by academic feminists using the analytical tools of poststructuralism.

In practice, sharing data analysis happened spontaneously in moments during a telephone conversation, in unplanned meetings in the local community, during friendly visits or just before or after a lesson. It also happened during class sessions, as I brought up themes or ideas that related to our class topics, drawing students into analytical discussions. I recorded and reflected on these informal conversations in my research diary. The collaboration was less systematic than I had originally envisaged and therefore the analysis belonged mostly to me, as the author of the project.

Conclusion

I have recounted the stages of the research process, emphasising that these were never distinct but always overlapping and impossible to fully control. I have examined the possibilities of a feminist poststructural ethnography for developing collaborative methodologies for the deconstruction and reconstruction of meaning. Poststructural theory was most useful as an analytical tool for addressing complexity, contradiction, difference and 'sameness' and for deconstructing competing discourses. The research also drew on structural analyses that address material inequality and work towards reconstructing politicised standpoints that struggle for justice.

I discovered the intricacies of the research process and the ways my contradictory and multiple subject positions overlapped, clashed and enriched each other. I considered the complex relationships that profoundly shaped the ethnography and the knowledge produced through it. It was not always possible to disrupt unequal power relations. All the participants felt vulnerable and exposed at times. It was my responsibility to decide which data to select and discard, so I needed to be reflexive about power and ethics. This entailed negotiating contradictory sets of interests and making decisions as the author-ity of the project in opposition to collaborative principles. As a complex process, collaboration was 'always on the edge of de-stabilizing' conventional power relations between researcher and researched, teacher and student (Hey, 2000:163). Therefore this ethnography created important moments but always temporary reconfigurations of power relations through collaborative attempts. The next chapter continues to explore themes of collaboration, inter-action and empowerment in relation to pedagogy.

4

The Role of Pedagogy in Widening Educational Participation

[Drawing on real life experiences] really helps because you have lots of examples from other people in the class and it makes it real. At the moment I feel I'm going in and just copying off the board – like at school. Just writing down and not really understanding – it reminds one of being at school. (Louise, 1999)

A close and reflexive examination of pedagogy is essential to any project that seeks to widen access. This chapter considers the effects of hegemonic discourses on teaching practices at Ford College. Feminist poststructural theory helps develop approaches to teaching and learning that are flexible according to context. This requires a deregulation of access teachers' pedagogical practices and a focus on the diverse perspectives of access students.

Critical and feminist pedagogy – from theory to practice
Access education has been influenced by critical pedagogy theory, which draws on the work of Paulo Freire (1972). His theory draws on his experience of teaching literacy to adults in South America and Africa (O'Malley, 1997). He argues that 'banking education', conventional education based on teacher authority and student passivity,

objectifies students, reinforcing the power and values of the oppressor. Freire believed that the oppressed were unaware of the true nature of social relationships under capitalism and that this 'false consciousness' helped oppressive social conditions and 'dehumanisation' to persist (Barr, 1999:14; Freire, 1972). The pedagogue should assist students in understanding the concrete conditions of their daily lives (Aronowitz, 1993: 9), a practice he called 'conscientization', the process of raising awareness of oppressive structures for political and collective action (Weiler, 1994: 17). The interaction through dialogue between the pedagogue and the oppressed will transform their knowledge of the world and this will lead to the utopian vision of liberation for all peoples.

Similarly, feminist approaches to pedagogy identified solidarity among the oppressed, based on women's shared experiences. Personal experiences were shared in consciousness-raising groups with the aim of constructing theory for political action. The goal was 'liberation', although feminists often failed to address their location in the very social relations they were attempting to challenge (Maher and Tetreault, 1994; Weiler, 1994: 33). Both Freirean and feminist theory produced a theoretical model of oppression positing a simple binary of power (oppressor-oppressed). The idea that once 'the oppressed' reach a level of rational enlightenment through conscientisation, all will work together to change the social world 'ignore[s] the possibility of the contradictory experience of oppression among the oppressed' (Barr, 1999: 15). Attempts to implement critical or feminist pedagogical theory without consideration of how both teacher and students are embedded in the very social inequalities and relationships they are attempting to disrupt perpetuates relations of domination (Johnson, 1997; Maher and Tetreault, 1994; Weiler, 1994:33; Ellsworth, 1992).

I experimented with critical pedagogy in the Qualitative Research Methods class, where the students were keen to collaborate with me. The idea was to develop my research methodology and the students' understanding of research processes, while also exploring the central themes of my research through our classroom practices. It highlighted the connections between my dual role as researcher and teacher and their dual role as students and participants. The experimental class provided an opportunity to consider links between methodology, pedagogy and practice with students. How could collaborative methodology contribute to the field of critical pedagogy and access education? I was strongly influenced by the collaborative work carried out by Ellsworth and her students (Ellsworth,1992).

Elizabeth Ellsworth writes about a course premised on collaboration with students, organised due to the increased racism at University of Wisconsin-Madison, where she is a professor. The course represented an attempt to intervene collectively 'against campus racism and traditional educational forms at the university' (Ellsworth, 1992: 90). The project investigated how racist structures and practices operated at the university, 'with what effects and contradictions – and where they were vulnerable to political opposition' (*ibid.*:92). Her paper describes the limitations and failure of critical pedagogy to cope practically with these aims. She concludes that critical pedagogy theory represents 'repressive myths' that perpetuate rather than transform relations of dominance. This is because it fails to locate itself within concrete practices, 'consistently strip[ping] discussions of classroom practices of historical context and political position' (*ibid.*:92).

The descriptor 'critical' is an example of the ambiguity characteristic of critical pedagogy theory, which conceals a political agenda by avoiding language such as anticlassism, antiracism and anti(hetero)sexism. This 'posture of invisibility' (*ibid.*) inhibits clear articulation of the need for political action through education. Her insights can be applied to the coded language used within access education – primarily with the term 'access', which implies a commitment to equal opportunities rather than a specific political agenda to challenge the masculinist, white and westernised world views privileged in and through the education system. This has enabled 'access education' to be expropriated into the initiative to widen participation, thus distorting a radical project into one that supports the political agenda of the New Right and the Third Way.

Ellsworth's paper inspired me to pursue collaborative approaches in the classroom and in my research, and to work with students to deconstruct the dominant discourses of teaching and learning. I wanted to test out whether or not *we* in the classroom felt that critical pedagogical approaches were experienced as repressive. I also wanted to explore the value of teacher-as-researcher projects, for the participants and the field of access education. I was reluctant to dismiss Freire's ideas as repressive without experimenting with them in practice. I suspected that critical pedagogical approaches would be experienced as both repressive *and* emancipatory.

Theorising complexities in classroom practices

One of the key concepts of critical pedagogy is that of 'student voice' (Ellsworth, 1992). It places importance on the idea of a student-centred approach in the classroom. Curriculum, pedagogy and materials are expected to be directly responsive to students' needs[1]. Teachers and researchers strive to 'make the voices of students' heard, with research committed to describing the experiences of students who have previously been excluded from educational opportunities (Merrill, 1996; Rosen, 1990; Moss, 1987). Such research has often been carried out along simplistic lines of gender or race, ignoring the ways that age, class, dis/ability, gender, race, and sexuality intersect, and neglecting the complexity of identity as multiple, fragmented, shifting and positional. This approach tends to ignore issues of selection, interpretation and the *social* process of constructing a 'voice' through available discourses.

Feminist poststructural theorists have critiqued categories of identity as fixed and final (e.g. 'woman' 'lesbian' 'white') because they build obstacles to creating possibilities for change (Mac an Ghaill and Haywood, 1997; Orner, 1992: 74) while maintaining the importance of these categories through the concept of positionality (Alcoff, 1988). The fixed, essential self of neo-liberal discourses ignores the complexities and fluidity of identity and power. Feminist poststructuralists attempt to engage with unconscious processes, pleasures and desires that we often deny or ignore, recognising that subjects are always in the process of 'becoming' and are constitutive of discourse (Orner, 1992: 79; Hall, 1992; see Chapter Six). The humanist concept of 'student voice' overlooks 'the mediating aspects of language and the unconscious' (Orner, 1992: 80; see also Ellsworth, 1997). Moreover, 'silence' does not always mean simply a loss of power or a position of oppression (Ellsworth, 1992; Orner, 1992). Students often actively choose to remain silent (although it is simplistic to translate silence into resistance). We need to move away from binaries such as silence/voice, oppressed/liberated, to address the micro-power relations that shape the intricate dynamics in classrooms.

As Valerie Walkerdine (1987) shows in her research on nursery-aged children, the pedagogical attempt to 'give voice' to 'the oppressed' does not take account of the complexities of classroom dynamics. Using an extract from a series of recordings made in a nursery classroom, she reveals the way 3 year-old boys can exercise power over their female teacher through 'constituting her as the powerless object of sexist discourse' (Walkerdine, 1987:167). Her research demonstrates that power does not operate in a simple dualism of powerful/powerless, in the way that critical pedagogy theory assumes. Teachers and students 'are not unitary subjects uniquely positioned, but produced as a nexus of subjectivities, in relations of power which are constantly shifting, rendering them at one moment powerful and at another powerless' (*ibid.*: 166).

Furthermore, Mimi Orner (1992) points out the danger of critical pedagogues believing themselves to be 'liberators' and 'givers of power'. Doing so ignores the ways they are situated and immersed in the same social formations and relationships as everyone else (Flax, 1995: 145) and also ignores the differential positions of power occupied by students. Instead, it places the teacher in the position of superior rescuer, single-handedly leading students to value themselves and make 'the right' choices. 'Stable notions of self and identity are based on exclusion' (Orner, 1992:86). The establishment of fixed categories within the classroom necessarily generates exclusions by coercing each student into a fixed category for fear of not belonging.

The positing of these conceptions such that only one perspective can be correct (or properly feminist) reveals, among other things, the embeddedness of feminist theory in the very processes we are trying to critique and our need for a more systematic and self-conscious theoretical practice. (Flax, 1995: 153)

Flax's point was made real when I asked students to discuss differences between women during a Women's Studies class. This extract from my research diary reveals some of the conflicts and anxieties that arose from my using feminist pedagogical approaches:

Difficult session...we split up into groups of three to discuss and consider differences between women. I overheard the discussion of one group, and one woman in particular, who was complaining that she did not agree with anything that had taken place in the class so far, that she could not relate to feminism at all and that she did not in any way feel that she was disadvantaged as a woman. [This was a woman who had earlier disclosed to the class that she had recently fled a violent marriage and was now struggling to raise her child on her own.] She sounded very angry with the other women in the class and complained that we had spoken about personal problems that she did not want to know about. I felt myself reacting to her words, and had to take deep breaths to calm down.

Later in the session when we reconvened, I said I had overheard some important issues being discussed about difference in one particular group, to prompt her to share her criticisms with the rest of the class. I said I hoped everyone felt they had a right to speak in the class, and that we would not all agree with each other all the time. Indeed this is what the session was about. She spoke up, explaining that she felt silenced because she seemed to feel differently to everyone else in the room. I responded by saying this was an example of why feminism must address difference between women. However, she then upset many women in the class by calling someone else 'stupid' for speaking about her personal experiences. I was so shocked at this verbal abuse that I did not directly respond. After the session, another student approached me and expressed her feeling that now we would all be too afraid to speak honestly about our experiences as women. (Friday, 16 October 1998)

My incapacity to defend the verbally abused student or to uphold the importance of autobiography illustrates that power dynamics constantly shift as subjects are constituted through discursive practices. This student employed the discourse of 'appropriate public behaviour' to shame other members of the group for stepping outside the boundaries of acceptable talk in a formal educational institution. I was included in her shaming, because I had behaved outside the discourse of professionalism and no longer signified the lecturer subject position. The discourse of feminist pedagogy was wholly disrupted and no one could rescue our feminist classroom practice that day.

Yet this story could be read differently. The discourse of feminism operated to silence this student who could or would not relate her personal experiences to the theoretical explanations of feminism(s). Feeling disconnected from the category 'feminist', she was silenced and marginalised by the pedagogical practices that I, as the teacher, had the power to impose on her in the classroom context. The narrative reveals the complexities of power relations, resistance and oppression. As Gore points out, it is crucial that teachers address the authority they exercise in their practice, because all pedagogical approaches circulate power that is potentially both emancipatory *and* repressive (Gore, 1993: 126). While teaching Women's Studies, I used my institutional position of authority as a source of power to develop what I hoped would be empowering practices to alter unequal classroom relations. However, it is clear that not all students at all times experienced the course as emancipatory. The complexities of power relations and discursive practices prompt teachers to re-examine the dilemmas facing critical classroom practice seriously and continually. Yet this does not undermine the importance of continuing to develop critical pedagogy for access education. It does emphasise the necessity *reflexively* to reconsider our ideas, practices, locations and relationships.

> In order to guard against the possibility that our own critical, feminist, social reconstructionist, or poststructuralist discourses would simply replace earlier discourses within the same institutions and disciplines, it is important to continuously and vigilantly carry

out the work of re-assembling, recommencement, critical renewal. (Gore, 1993: 155)

Mainstream discourses of widening educational participation

While feminist and critical theorists have struggled with the concept of pedagogy, it has been increasingly absent from the dominant discourse of widening participation. As the market is increasingly prioritised in education (Power and Whitty, 1999; Kenway and Epstein, 1996), concerns with pedagogy become lost through an overwhelming concern with standards. The Secretary of State for Education and Employment argues that 'Standards are at the very heart of creating equality' (Blunkett, 8 March 1999), and the Chief Executive of QAA asserts that 'Access matters because standards matter' (Randall, 1998).

Over recent years, widening educational participation has become a key issue in national policy, guided by the Government's incentive to modernise the welfare state:

> Learning is essential to a strong economy and an inclusive society. In offering a way out of dependency and low expectation, it lies at the heart of the Government's welfare reform programme. (DfEE, February 1998: 11)

The market principles of neo-liberalism have moulded this incentive. Widening participation is using 'education' as a gateway from benefits to employment. The emphasis is on Basic and Key Skills to improve the standard of the British workforce. In Chapter Two, I explored the possible implications of this emphasis. It also affects pedagogical practices, leading to utilitarian kinds of competence-based teaching and learning (Johnson, 1997), while constraining possibilities for anticlassist, anti(hetero)sexist and antiracist pedagogy.

The hegemonic discourse focuses on individual responsibility, encapsulated in the Government's initiative of 'education for citizenship' (DfEE, June 1999). This use of 'citizenship' differs from that in access education. In access education, 'citizenship' relates to critical thinking and analysis to help students participate actively in social transformation (Mayo, 1997: 124). In the neo-liberal discourse, citizenship is related to individual rights and responsibilities (*ibid.*: 123). This is illustrated by the Education Secretary's words:

> Through raising standards in education and a strong focus on citizenship we can achieve our vision. That is why self-reliance, self-determination and mutual support are all part of the same endeavour, to use the talents of the individuals to the benefits of the whole community. (Blunkett, 8 March 1999; see also DfEE, February, 1998).

Individual rights and responsibilities are linked to concerns with the national economy. Throughout policy documents, widening participation is regarded as investing in human capital:

> Investment in human capital will be key to business success in the knowledge-based economy of the 21st century, Education and Employment Secretary David Blunkett said today. Mr Blunkett said there is now a real challenge to quantify investment in human skill and creativity. He called on the accountancy profession and investment analysts to take a lead in devising new ways of measuring knowledge and creativity, not just plant and equipment. Speaking at the annual public lecture of the Centre for Policy Studies in Education at the University of Leeds, Mr Blunkett said: 'Knowledge is now wealth and power. Microsoft is so valuable, not because of its fixed assets, but because of the human capital of its software engineers and programmers. Each of its employees is 'worth' about £6.6 million... It is not only individuals but businesses that must embrace a learning culture which will be the key to developing human capital. This will be about partnerships – Government, business and individuals pooling resources together – to underline the importance of learning, which today is the key to employability, job security and higher earnings'. (DfEE, 11 March 1999)

The neo-liberal discourse undermines 'why and for whom we wish to widen participation' (Diamond, 1999: 188). It has pushed issues of pedagogy to the background of discussions that instead prioritise standards, systems and frameworks.

From the margins to the centre

The successful transition of access education from the margins of post-compulsory education to the centre of national policy deserve recognition and celebration. Now a programme with national currency and status, Access to Higher Education is regulated by the Quality Assurance Agency for Higher Education (QAA). This development, combined with other changes, has altered the discourse of widening participation.

The access movement was initially driven by a commitment to redress the balance set by the legacy of institutional classism, racism and sexism. Feminist, antiracist and anti(hetero)sexist pedagogical approaches were central to many Access to Higher Education programmes striving to widen participation. Responding to local and heterogeneous needs, access education was practitioner led (Clarke, 1999; Maxwell, 1996). The approach to access education:

> meant that provision could be designed to meet local needs and be responsive both to the expertise of staff and to the local communities in which provision was based. It allowed for Access programmes to be linked to local HE institutions or be separate from them. It allowed for varieties in the organisation of the curriculum and for experimentation in the way programmes were constructed. *In particular, it specifically rejected the conventional A-level approach to teaching and learning.* In those early days, part of the dialogue between Access practitioners focused on the extent to which Access was a means to effect change within HE itself. (Diamond, 1999: 186; emphasis added)

The early to mid 1990s saw a huge expansion in Access to Higher Education (Clarke, 1999; Diamond, 1999: 186). This was triggered by the legitimisation of Access through the arrival of the kitemark (Diamond: 1999: 186). The subsequent unitisation of Access modules enabled providers to select 'off-the-peg modules', but it also moved Access practitioners away from flexibility and responsiveness to local needs (*ibid.*). Such changes have resulted in the regulation and control of Access provision, culminating in appointment of the QAA to oversee it. Although this has strengthened the Access programme in some ways, the emphasis on standards and standardisation has constrained innovative approaches to pedagogy, shifting the focus to frameworks and structures.

Standardising Assessment

In a recent OCN conference (NELAF OCN, 20 May 1999), standards were the theme of the day. One of the workshops focused exclusively on standardisation of assessment. A consensus was quickly established, pointing up the value of transparency in assessment systems. Teachers, delegates agreed, should set out the aims and objectives of the assessment exercise clearly in checksheet form, a method largely adopted by City and Guilds courses. The student has a list of points s/he must cover, and the teacher ticks off the boxes to assess the student. If all the boxes are ticked, the student has passed and 'proven' their competence at a particular level.

When a conference delegate pointed out how prescriptive this approach might be, the group ignored her point and detracted from it. There was collective refusal to engage in a reflexive discussion about 'transparency' and to address the complexities of the issues involved. Transparency once meant a political commitment to challenge the elitist mysticism surrounding academia. Conventional assessment strategies were critiqued for re-privileging groups with the cultural capital to decode obscure academic language. But now transparency has been appropriated to support the move towards standardisation. This stunts the development of innovative pedagogy that directly addresses the diverse needs and interests of marginalised groups.

The term transparency conceals that all texts are socially constructed and are read by different subjects in different ways. Just as Usher claims that 'researchers are never fully the 'authors' of their texts' (1997: 26), neither are a group of educationalists preparing a set of assessment criteria fully the 'authors' of their texts. If 'different languages, different registers of the same language, different discourses each construct the world differently; if, in effect, different worlds are 'knowledged' or 'languaged' into being' (Usher, 1997: 29) then what happens when a panel of educators 'language' a different world to the world 'languaged' by the student? One student's awareness of such complexities surfaced when we were discussing an interview schedule for my PhD research:

> *Helen made a very perceptive point about setting questions in the interview. She said the interviews would not necessarily produce 'relevant' answers for my research because participants might answer questions in a totally different way to what I had expected and interpret what I say differently from what I thought I meant.*
> (Research diary, 23 February, 1999)

Obviously Helen was talking about a separate issue; interview questions in a research project. However, the insight she provides here helps to clarify the issue of transparency and assessment checksheets. The checksheet may appear to be transparent to the teacher who has written it; however her/his meanings may be misinterpreted by the students reading it. This throws the notion of transparency into question. It also suggests, promisingly, that there are always gaps for subversive misreadings of the author-itative texts guiding pedagogical practices.

Bronwell Maxwell traces two main areas of change within the Open College Network (OCN). The first is the exponential growth in the number of OCN-recognised courses and the number of students gaining OCN credits. The second is the heavy usage of the OCN by the FE sector to gain unit recognition and accredit mainstream provision (Maxwell, 1996: 111). This has created a situation where:

- the flexibility and responsiveness of OCNs in accrediting adult learners' achievements, particularly in the area of informal and semi-formal learning, will be severely reduced

- recognition of adults' learning will be dependent on their moving through externally determined, pre-specified 'boxes'. Was it ever the intention to dismantle the long haul from the bottom of the educational 'ladder', only to replace it with a set of boxes?

- the role of adult learners in formulating their own learning programmes will be reduced

- informal learning will be once again marginalised and undervalued in the education sector

- the aim of widening participation will not be achieved, as the diversity of provision at the first stages of returning to learning is reduced

- many small community groups will be excluded from gaining accreditation for their learning, and will therefore lose opportunities for progression

- OCNs will be driven not by a mission to meet the needs of adult learners but by institutional and organisational aims. (Maxwell, 1996: 112)

Maxwell provides a map of OCN development that reveals a fundamental shift. The concern to address the diversity of student needs has been replaced with a universal top-down model. Maxwell sharply articulates the problem:

> What is deeply worrying about the changing approach to quality assurance is that it represents a radical shift from a credit system designed around meeting the actual needs and situations of adult learners, to awarding credits only if the needs and situations of adult learners are compatible with the accreditation system. (*ibid.*)

A focus on assessment standardisation detracts from pedagogical concerns. Standardised assessment approaches reinstate dominant 'regimes of truth' and particular classroom cultures premised on racist and sexist formations. The criteria reinforce culture-specific ways of writing, arguing and thinking. Answers outside of conventional academic discourses are seen as invalid. This is illustrated in my diary:

> *Helen explained how frustrated she felt about the Access course at the moment. Not the teachers, but the whole structure of the course. Particularly the ways she was forced to write. And when she didn't do as well as she hoped on assessed work, this reinforced her lack of self-confidence and negative self-perceptions. The whole class agreed with everything she said. Peter said it was an absolute struggle to write in the expected way, and that it felt almost*

impossible. Helen said there was one particular class that frustrated her most because, although they had discussions, the questions were pre-set in a way that heavily restricted and anticipated their responses. Their responses seemed to be pre-determined. (Research diary, 9 March 1999)

Although the Access teacher, described above, attempts to have an open discussion, this is undermined by the assessment criteria, which determines how the discussion is framed and prescribes the responses required from students in order to produce 'correct' answers. Student challenges to hegemonic discourses seem highly unlikely if not impossible. Although the teacher desires a generative open discussion with students, the regulative, pre-set criteria have undermined her attempts. She is constrained by the available and acceptable constructs of 'teacher', and students are restricted by the dominant meanings of 'student'. The narrow focus on standards and standardisation reproduces dominant discourses and marginalises radical discourses.

Johnson-Riordan (1997) usefully develops the concept of a 'colonising discourse'. This signifies the exclusionary strategy that serves to further alienate those already on the margins. This illuminates the processes described by Helen, which lead to the marginalisation of students' contributions to epistemological debates.

Johnson-Riordan also introduces the idea of 'de-colonising' education, focusing on Sociology and the authoritarian nature of its texts. Calling for the rewriting of narratives, categories and frameworks of mainstream sociology, she proposes an exploration of useful 'border crossings' between disciplinary boundaries. This is a particularly helpful approach for Access to Higher Education, which offers a variety of subject areas but often does not enable students to make interconnections between and through subject divisions. During my work as an access teacher, external moderator and researcher, many students have told me that moving across and between disciplines helps their understanding and engagement in their learning, whereas having to approach disciplines as separate areas has hampered their grasping abstract ideas.

Johnson-Riordan asks us to rework the separate spheres of teaching and research, which idea is central to this book. If we think of classroom work as *research* as well as teaching, we will develop reflexive skills and increase our ability to deal with contextual issues and difference. If we move beyond *method* and focus on *methodology* and *pedagogy*, we approach teaching as a creative and interactive process and relationship. In collaboration with students, we research classroom dynamics reflexively to develop and reconstruct pedagogy that is responsive to context. As Richard Johnson (1997: 45) argues, 'we must contrive and must sustain critical self-reflexive dialogues about educational aims and practices', including exchanges between teachers and dialogue with students. It is important to discuss how, why and what we teach (*ibid.*: 55) and how all this relates to wider social structures, formations of oppression, hegemonic discourses and unequal power relations. We need also to make connections between these wider contexts and the micro-contexts in which our classrooms are located.

Autobiography as a pedagogical tool

Autobiography helps explore the interconnections between social structures, power relations, discursive practices and the private world of knowing and meaning. It is a tool for examining 'the social within each individual' and the ways that 'knowledge structures [are] retold in the individual's own life stories' (*ibid.*). Autobiography, as a form of 'cultural critique' (Miller cited in Johnson-Riordan, 1997:125) is a useful pedagogical strategy in the project to 'engage in reclaiming culture, difference, subjectivities, borders and memories against the colonising discourse which poses itself as universal and ignores difference'.

Conventional academic approaches exclude and reject the body, subjectivity and experience as sites of knowledge. Yet, exploring the personal and autobiographical is essential to the deconstruction of dominant discourses, to make sense of how they shape social meanings and our identity positions.

Autobiography opens possibilities for radical discourses. It generates alternative readings, to recreate new meanings and narratives against the grain of common sense and privileged knowledge (Johnson-Riordan, 1997:125). Through sharing personal stories, reading, discussion and analytical thinking, theory may be collaboratively reconstructed within the classroom.

In this discussion, students consider the importance of the personal in their learning:

> Shelley: *Well, I found Women's Studies more stimulating and more enjoyable umm, just by, by learning from other people, the other pupils have been able to contribute themselves.*
>
> PB: *Mmm...so you found it, you found it, umm, rewarding to actually share ideas.*
>
> Shelly: *Yeah, yeah and to be allowed to share ideas and – and have them respected.*
>
> Kate: *It comes from the heart ...it helps you to read life.*
>
> (Women's Studies group interview, 1999)

Similar themes emerge from the Women's Group discussion:

> Lynsey: *I do feel stronger since Women's Studies.*
>
> PB: *In what ways?*
>
> Lynsey: *Confidence and everything. Like doing that other course... [the tutor] said, 'well out of all the class, you've written the most'. And I said 'well aren't you supposed to do that – to think for yourself'. Because they put the answers at the back of the book. So you're not thinking. So I'm looking at the answers to get ideas, but trying to put in my own answers as well.*
>
> Kate: *I found that difficult. Because my answers were really coming from here [she points to her heart], but when I looked at the answers it was coming from logic and it wasn't about logic, it was about feelings.*
>
> (Women's Group discussion, December 1999)

The theme of the personal as significant in developing critical thinking reoccurs throughout my research diary. For example:

Today the subject focus was on 'the family and mothering', but we tended to keep moving into broader political areas as well as personal examples of the relevant issues. The class discussed the importance of moving freely in and out of the formal course agenda and how inter-connected the personal was to the theoretical as well as the political. Students commented that the 'free' discussion was much richer than the tight boundaries of 'legitimate knowledge'. Kate said 'everything becomes clear to me when I'm at college on Friday mornings' and stressed her increasing feelings of validation in terms of her own emotions and experiences. (Research diary, 6 May 1999)

Using autobiography does not mean confusing education with individual therapy or a confessional discourse. Autobiography is a resource, to be used in combination with analysis, reflexivity, theory, reading and deconstruction. Such a combined strategy helps to challenge discourses which claim to be universal and 'correct' and to work towards a 'liberation of the mind' (Professor Gloria Wade-Gayles, Emory University quoted in Maher and Tetreault, 1994: 175). However, the aim is not to build new regimes of truths which will only serve to disempower 'other others', so it is vital to reflexively connect theory, subjectivity, experience, contextuality and the reconstruction of meaning.

There are no simple 'how to' recipes for collaborative pedagogy, although interactive approaches are particularly valuable.

The interactive classroom

The interactive classroom rejects the model of teacher-as-expert and keeper of all truth. The student is regarded as a source of knowledge, and collaboration between teacher and learner is central to the pedagogy. Interactive approaches include small group discussions, class brainstorms, autobiographical and journal writing, sharing personal stories, text-based workshops, pair discussions, brief talks and collaborative evaluations. The interactive classroom rejects the lecture as the main conveyor of knowledge and repudiates the notion that there is one correct answer (Epstein, 1997: 182). Interaction reduces 'the distance between the expertise of the lecturer and the apprenticeship of the student' and validates students' knowledge while making the teachers' knowledge provisional (*ibid.*).

> Greg: *People can say what they want to say and you should listen to that because you can learn from anyone. You don't just learn from the teacher; you can learn from someone that you haven't heard speak before.*
>
> PB: *That's right...*
>
> Greg: *They can say something you just haven't thought about and go, oh gawd yeah, that's so right!*
>
> (Return to Study group discussion, 1999)

All the participants affirmed the value of learning from other students:

> PB: *Do you think having life experiences helped your learning at all?*
>
> Hilda: *I think so, I think it has. Umm, and I think for me personally, because of what I'd been through with my husband and the people I'd seen through his illness, I'd begun to realise that there are lots of people who aren't as fortunate as I am and I think that continued at college, and I had to try very hard to be understanding and patient. 'Cause I'm very quick to think everybody should understand more and be capable and I think it was umm, quite interesting for me to have to think about these other people and how different they were and their different backgrounds. Which I don't think you'd be capable of as a younger person without experience...*
>
> PB: *So it made you realise that people were at different points and they've all had different backgrounds...*
>
> Hilda: *...and different levels, but they are all still valid.*
>
> PB: *Did you learn from those people?*
>
> Hilda: *Definitely! Definitely. That's quite huge really.*
>
> (Hilda, 1999)

Hilda is able to draw on personal experiences to challenge discourses that invalidate working-class ideas and she recognises that this will be a major resource for learning.

However, the interactive approach has its problems. Bringing personal experiences into the classroom is risky and has the potential to reproduce unequal power relations. Revealing painful experiences and vulnerable aspects of one's identity often increases feelings of powerlessness and inferiority. This is why reflexivity in interactive pedagogy is a crucial tool for addressing the complexity of localised power relationships. Collaborative research and pedagogy facilitated reflexive processes. Nevertheless, this did not ensure that problems were solved; rather it opened up awareness to the complexity of power. In the following extract I am speaking with a student about his experiences of our experimental Research Methods course.

> John: *I – you could see people evolving within themselves and coming to their own conclusions through their interaction with other people, you know, things like that, so it was very beneficial I would say.*

> PB: *I was aware that there were some students who weren't participating as actively and that concerned me a lot. Umm, I mean, were you aware of that?*

> John: *I was aware of that, I was very aware of that and...I mean I was eager, you know, I'd found something at last. But I'd become sensitive to that fact and uh I do believe in time those students, given time they would have been able to express themselves you know. Because in a situation like that, when they see other people being open, and being honest and as truthful as they can be, I'm sure that would have, you know, rubbed off on them and they would have seen it as an opportunity for them to then express themselves.*

Sharing personal stories can be empowering pathways to resistance and theory reconstruction but it can also be risky. The disclosure of personal experiences may leave students and teachers feeling vulnerable. An understanding that stories can be risky helps participants to explore power relationships in and outside the classroom. It is also important to recognise that stories change over time, even as they become fixed stories we tell about who we think we are. These are not objective truths but subjective constructions. Such recognition provides an insight into the construction of subjectivities and the ways they are classed, gendered, raced and sexualised. It also points to the ways our subjectivities are constituted through shifting and contradictory discourses. Such pedagogical practices 'assert students' multiplicity of voices, but also deconstruct them, see how they have become what they are, challenge problematic sexist and racist assumptions within them, and reconstruct them' (Hernández, 1997: 20).

Border crossings in the Access classroom

The interactive classroom reveals the interconnections between autobiography, experience, theory, concept and narrative. The final section of this chapter draws on a recorded group discussion with three Access to Higher Education students. We are exploring the importance of making interconnections in the classroom. The students led the discussion into a reflection of another class held earlier that day, where they were asked to think about sexism.

> Leslie: *Like today...what were we doing today...we were doing sexism... but I found the lesson quite unstimulating – I found myself rebelling and when they were discussing about women and what they dressed like and should women, like, wear short skirts and we were just talking about fashion, weren't we. And how, you know, if women conform to that and I was like you know [laugh] this is a load of bollix... people wear what they want to. Do you know what I mean? What does it matter if women want to wear feminine things. And I just couldn't get past all that, you know...*

> John: *Yeah, it's just that the context of the debate was completely wrong. It was just left on a surface level as it were. It was just like, banter, really, you know? So that's why you didn't get hooked.*

> Leslie: *I find it really boring. I found it really hard and I wasn't taking up anything today...because like you said, of course I'm interested in women's issues, but today I just couldn't be bothered with anything 'cause it's all like superficial stuff.*

Leslie claims they were 'doing' sexism. The verb 'doing' signifies her pedagogical assumption that concepts such as 'sexism' are blocks of knowledge that can be 'done'. Students passively assimilate the teacher's explanation, memorise it, and then demonstrate this knowledge in the assessment process. It is an example of Freire's concept of 'banking education'. The students regard such passive approaches as 'superficial' learning. Their frustration relates to the discouragement of an active engagement with the concept 'sexism'. They sense that they are not benefiting intellectually or personally from such classroom experience. There is an implicit awareness that learning of this kind is not transformative.

The students continued to explain how the class discussion failed to make vital connections between their experiences, their gendered identities and the active construction of theory and meaning.

> Leslie: *I think that what pissed me off really was...when she was listing things on the board about women's role, I was like, do we not all know this? I felt it was like ...of course we know what identifies a woman's role. Of course we know things like that! Do you know what I mean? There isn't a person in the class who couldn't tell you what gender roles mean, surely. Surely! But what's important isn't the gender roles, its why they're there in the first place.*

> Helen: *I've probably come up against sexist remarks in the past. If we talked about that...*

> PB: *Its also that if you made links between women's lives in the 50s and 60s and their struggle and how that actually affected your lives today...*

> Helen: *But like how we've just talked about sexism, if we had done that, we should, we should have been able to do that earlier on today. We would have got a lot more out of it. Nothing against the teacher. It's just that if we were allowed to bring up our own ideas, and relate it to something then I'd understand it. Go away and do something with it. Or not. But now, you just can't.*

Leslie identifies why the class discussion felt superficial: they never reached the heart of the issue. '*But what's important isn't the gender roles, its why they're there in the first place.*' Under the heading 'gender roles', the class brainstormed women's expected social roles, without exploring why this list was significant to their own gendered identities and the maintenance of social inequalities. The list was meaningless and patronising to a group of adult students who had vivid experiences of unequal gender relations. There was no opportunity to draw on their experiences to consider, deconstruct and refashion knowledge about the significance of sexism and gender.

Pedagogy matters

This chapter highlighted the ways my dual position of teacher-as-researcher enabled the co-participants collaboratively to examine pedagogy in relation to their classroom experiences. The collaborative approach uncovered compelling connections between methodology, epistemology, pedagogy and practice.

It is important to revitalise discussions about the relationship between pedagogy and educational access by focusing on the diverse insights and experiences of students. Feminist poststructural theory exposes the complexity of pedagogical relations, processes and practices. The absence of pedagogical debates within current policy and practice has major implications for widening participation. The commitment to widening participation is largely driven by concerns to modernise the welfare state, linking welfare to 'education' as a bridge to work. This approach, tied to market principles, constructs access students as consumers of lifelong learning, which has in turn led to an emphasis on competition and to utilitarian kinds of competence-based learning. The focus on standards and standardisation has moved us away from innovative pedagogy.

The following chapter explores the students' narratives of intimidation. It reveals how hegemonic discourses reposition access students as inferior and shows how the participants resist this by creating radical spaces in their access classrooms.

Notes

1 The concept of 'needs' relates to specific social groups, e.g. mature women students. This is problematic because it reconfirms differences based on essentialist meanings associated with 'being a woman'. Riley argues that while struggling for the 'needs' of women is important, we must do so 'by keeping it clear that these demands represent only current and not universal needs of women' (Riley, 1983: 194-195 cited in Alcoff, 1988: 428).

5

Intimidating Education

I felt really nervous and sick and when I walked into the college the first time I thought what am I doing here? (Linda, 1999)

Coming back to college was nerve-racking! (Louise, 1999)

The participants' narratives reveal feelings of intimidation and inferiority in terms of their educational experiences. This chapter examines these expressions of anxiety in relation to non-traditional learning.

Intimidation is a big thing!

There's a fear of being in the classroom. Intimidation; that's a big thing. (Kerry, 1999)

Access education targets social groups whom have historically been excluded from education. Yet, access students are required to enter an arena that is often seen as the property of the middle classes. Educational space is historically a colonialist and patriarchal domain regulated through class privilege (Morley, 1999: 87; Bird, 1998; Fieldhouse, 1996:2; Evans, 1995; Purvis, 1991: 117 – 118; Acker and Piper, 1990). Although access education challenges inequality and exclusion, it is located in an institution founded on classist, sexist and racist traditions.

However, the academic world has transformed significantly over the past century and continues to change in a new age of uncertainty.

Education is now a quasi-market and can no longer be simplistically described as patriarchal or elitist (although new and more complex power relations have developed as a consequence). The educational consumer is not discriminated against on the basis of gender, as women may constitute a lucrative market to target for inclusion. But as Mary Evans argues 'universities can recognise a lucrative, gendered market but then ignore the particular gendered needs of that group' (1995: 74). Research shows that within higher education, class privilege is maintained and women's participation is limited to the bottom end of a hierarchical continuum (Morley, 1999: 178; Gardiner and O'Rourke, 1998: 133-134; Evans, 1995: 73; Davies and Holloway, 1995: 12; Bagilhole, 1994: 15; Fryer, 1990: 280).

The industrialisation of education

Post-compulsory education has been marketised and moved into a mass system. Indeed, the shift from an elite to a mass system has enabled the Access to Higher Education programme to map out its own distinct space within the mainstream educational landscape. Mass higher education is assumed to mean that all sections of the population are equally represented in higher education. Statistical evidence reveals that this is not a true picture (NOCN annual report, 1997-8; Leonard, 1994: 164; Egerton and Halsey, 1993: 189). Evans argues that mass education simply means that more middle class women are now participating in higher education (Evans, 1995:74).

Although women's access to education has opened up to some extent – keeping in mind that class, dis/ability and ethnicity also come into play – little has changed in terms of curriculum content and organisation (ibid.; Shuster, 1994: 197). As Morley comments, 'the demographic composition of the academy is changing, while organisational cultures seem to be lagging behind' (1999: 87). The academy has legitimated specific ways of studying the world while proscribing others (Evans, 1995). This has served to privilege white, masculinist and Westernised perspectives, ideologies and values; for example that there are universal answers, that knowledge should centre on the public world and that 'emotion' belongs outside of intellectual pursuits (*ibid.*). These academic approaches have been claimed as objective and value-free, although challenged by critical scholarship. Dominant discourses of the academy are entwined with the hegemony of neo-liberalism and neo-colonialism. Anne Ryan argues that these discourses, combined with a mass system, position 'non-traditional' students as 'other', marking them with the status of 'outsider'. The hegemony of neo-liberalism has led to a situation in which the 'mental space in which people dream is largely occupied by Western imagery' (Sachs 1992: 4 cited in Ryan, 2000: 46).

> Within the higher education sector to date there is evidence of a marked preference for maintaining the existing educational delivery system and little evidence of a willingness to critique the knowledge base that informs this system. Participation in the system is conditional on conformity to predetermined truths and dissention is suppressed. (Ryan, 2000: 51)

Others warn that the mass education system has created the industrialisation of education:

> Indeed for others, democratic participation in higher education is a contradiction in terms. Universities cannot function effectively as centres of intellectual production if they are overrun by students. Some colleagues draw parallels with the effects of mass tourism on National Parks and similar amenities. For them, increased student numbers and the pursuit of diverse income sources are leading to the *industrialisation of education*, where the mass production of graduates and credentials is replacing the carefully hand-crafted scholar of a former era. (HEQC, 1994: 329 quoted in Morley, 1999: 142)

Another problem with the mass system is the 'very pressure of numbers resulting from the market success of attracting and accepting' students who have not reached higher education through conventional courses (Epstein, 1995: 61). Epstein asks:

> To what extent can the extension of access to Higher Education be said to have improved equal opportunities if many of the students entering HE for the first time lack the tools which will enable them to succeed in gaining degrees and are not enabled to gain those tools? (*ibid.*)

With increasing pressures on tutors to juggle a range of responsibilities, challenging institutional inequalities may sometimes feel
like an impossible goal (Morley, 1999: 143; Epstein, 1995; Skeggs,
1995a). Students are all too aware of the hardships tutors face in
their multifaceted roles, generating sympathy from students despite
the personal disappointment that their needs are consequently not
being met.

Class, gender and the discourses of mass education

Mass education has been interpreted from a variety of discourse
positions (Williams, 1997a; Ball, 1990). The 'academic traditiona-
lists' (Ball, 1990) regard the mass system as undermining the tried
and tested elite system of provision. This discourse position has
generated a moral panic around standards (Williams, 1997a: 31).
Elite is equated with 'quality' and mass with 'second-class'.

> The notion of 'mass' within this position resonates with labels of
> 'cheap and nasty', with a cultural discourse within which 'the
> masses' is a term of denigration and mass production cannot be
> quality production. (*ibid.*: 32)

What Ball (1990) calls the 'marketeers' advocate a market-led approach to education, arguing that 'a mass market provides for
entrepreneurial potential and a cheaper product but an elite sector
can and should remain as differentiated consumers demand a differentiated product' (*ibid.*: 35). This position justifies that presti-
gious institutions 'remain the cultural possession of the traditionally
advantaged' (Williams, 1997b: 158). These institutions draw on the
discourse of academic excellence in order to protect their interests in
maintaining an elitist system (*ibid.*).

The notion of mass education is contested, and precisely whom it
benefits is also debatable. For example, Woodrow (1996: 6) argues:

> A mass system of higher education is not for the masses. In a
> period when recession and regressive economic policies have
> widened the gap between the rich and poor, we have not suc-
> ceeded in tackling under representation caused by socio-economic
> status. The virtual extinction of discretionary awards, changes in

social security, the sharp decline in the real value of grants, and the unresolved shambles of student loan schemes have increasingly shifted responsibility for funding on to students and their families. This has resulted in a system of access by ability to pay. (cited in Williams, 1997b: 160)

Non-standard students

'A' levels are still regarded as the gold standard and 'the normal method of entry, the signifier of both individual and institutional worth, the predictor of quality output' (*ibid.*: 160; see also Thompson, 1997: 114; Leonard, 1994: 174).

It is against these standards that access students are judged as less worthy. They are automatically categorised as 'non-standard' because they have not taken the traditional 'A' level route at age 18 (Webb, 1997: 68). Terms such as 'non-standard' carry meanings relating to age, class, ethnicity, gender and race (Williams, 1997b).

The majority of my research participants saw college as a place where they do not belong. Participants strongly identified with the 'non-standard' category. Working-class identities rendered them outsiders in the academic realm, while lecturers and traditional students were regarded as legitimate, possessing 'real' knowledge.

> Like I said before, about being at school, I think you get this impression of the teacher being better than you. (Linda, 1999)

Participants' accounts suggested that to be working-class is be practical and not intellectual, and to never 'get it right':

> Categories of class operate not only as an organising principle which enable access to and limitations on social movement and interaction but are also reproduced at the intimate level as a 'structure of feeling' in which doubt, anxiety and fear inform the production of subjectivity. To be working-classed, Kuhn (1995) argues, generates a constant fear of never having 'got it right'. (Skeggs, 1997: 6)

As Kerry writes in her student diary:

> First day back after the summer holidays. What a shock!! I didn't expect Sociology to get so heavy so quickly. The teacher seems like

an approachable guy thank god, because I will probably be going
to him for lots of help. **Question: Why do I always feel that I am**
not good enough to do the work? *Answer: I don't know. I must*
look into it. (Kerry, 1999, emphasis added)

These expressions of inferiority are rooted in a history and cultural
common sense in which working-class groups, particularly women,
have been seen as potentially pathological and polluting. Stanley
articulates this clearly:

> The knowledge/power structures that impact at an individual level
> are the product of social and economic systems that have for cen-
> turies excluded people of my gender, my class and those margina-
> lized by 'race', age and bodily disabilities. Language is used to
> signify and reinforce class oppression; formal education institutions
> are just examples of the places where systematic shaming and
> undermining, posited on notions of superiority and inferiority, are re-
> inforced. That eroding phrase 'working-class thicko' no longer even
> needs to be spoken, so well is it internalized. It is a conditioned res-
> ponse, quite fixed before adolescence (transmitted through
> advertising and media as well as through school and social inter-
> actions), and one which is useful to a society which wants working-
> class women to take a usefully low and unchallenging position
> within it. (1995: 171)

An extended concept of the 'hidden curriculum' helps to explain
such processes within educational institutions. The hidden curriculum signifies the implicit process of learning through the general
ethos or environment of a school or college (Epstein, 1995: 57).
Epstein expands the concept to account for the wider political, historical and social contexts that determine how the teacher and
student make sense of the taught curriculum:

> We can think of the curriculum (taught and hidden) as a kind of text
> (in its extended sense) which students are required to read. In this
> context we can see that how students 'read' the curriculum (or what
> they learn) derives from a combination of what lecturers offer (and
> the way they offer it), the ethos produced by the institutional
> arrangements of particular classes and of the institution as a whole,
> and events and common senses from the wider society. In other

words, the hidden curriculum can be seen as including the cultural referents available to students and staff alike. (*ibid.*: 59)

Examining the construction of social class and gender helps to explain the way context, culture, subjectivity and social space combine to form a dynamic hidden curriculum.

Exploring the historical context

Kerry describes the sense of inferiority she cannot explain. Morley notes that:

> Anna Freud (1937) suggested that subordinate and oppressed parties tend to introject, or internalise, the negative characteristics that their oppressors have projected on to them. This interpretation acknowledges the extent to which misinformation as a result of racism, sexism, classism, heterosexism and disablism has been internalised by subordinated groups. (Morley, 1999: 113)

Once we deconstruct the dominant narratives about working-class women the discourses to which Kerry is subject become clear. It is through the inherited legacy of working-class women's presumed 'unworthiness' that Kerry comes to see herself as 'not good enough to do the work'. If we consider the history of the patriarchal discourse of the 'inferior working-class woman', the connection between the social construction and the personal expression of (lack of) self-value made by Kerry is revealed.

The bourgeois domestic ideology became established during the nineteenth century transition from an aristocratic, capitalist society to an industrial, capitalist society. Purvis (1987:253) highlights three assumptions of this ideology. First, there is a natural division between men and women expressed through the separation of the public and private spheres. Second, women are not independent individuals but are defined in relation to men and children. Third, women are naturally inferior to men. Such assumptions were supported by biological determinism and the religious idea of a divine natural order.

> Biological differences between the sexes and the supposed inferiority of woman's intellect were used too as arguments to oppose the entry of women into higher education in the 1860s and after. (*ibid.*: 254)

Although all women were tied to this ideology, the bourgeoisie upheld ideals of femininity that were class-specific. 'They upheld a double standard in that what was considered appropriate, relevant and attainable for middle-class women was inappropriate, irrelevant and unattainable for working-class women' (*ibid.*: 255).

The ideal form of femininity, that of the 'perfect wife and mother', involved the display of certain virtues such as self-denial, patience, resignation and the ability to manage a household without engaging in manual labour. Working-class women could only aspire to the secondary 'good woman' status, as housekeeper, wife and mother. Held responsible for stabilising the feared working-class family, the working-class woman was identified as both the solution to and the cause of numerous social problems (Skeggs, 1997: 76).

The working-class family was used as an explanation (and excuse) for social disharmony and malfunction (*ibid.*). Working-class women were frequently blamed for social problems including alcoholism, crime, the spread of disease and a high infant mortality rate (Purvis, 1987: 256). Those problems associated with industrialisation and urbanisation were projected onto the working-class woman and her supposed failure to fulfil her role as a 'good woman'. These bourgeois judgements and ideals formed part of the context within which educational institutions were founded and reformed – those who formulated policy were mainly from the middle classes (*ibid.*: 257)

This historical legacy can still be traced within education today, expressed for example through the discourse of selection (Williams, 1997a). As was evident in the competing explanations of mass education, opening the educational gates to the working classes is often regarded as detrimental to the maintenance of high standards and quality. This continues...

> University proper is for a tiny elite. The expansion of Britain's universities has led (as predicted) to disastrous confusion, disappointment and a collapse of standards. In the name of meritocracy, most universities ought to be closed down, or be converted into genuinely vocational tertiary colleges. (Minette Marrin, 1999, *The Daily Telegraph*)

It is seen as commendable in a 'fair' meritocratic system for academic gatekeepers to 'allow' in individuals who can prove their special talent (by default this means the special individuals who do not have birthrights to the middle class privilege of attending university). However, this is considered a dangerous move when particular social groups (rather than talented *individuals* from particular social groups) are targeted for inclusion, since this may alter the fragile 'natural order' and therefore national social stability. Again, Marrin encapsulates this position:

> It is worth remembering that meritocracy is a dangerous genie to let out of the bottle. Meritocracy is always invoked in the name of fairness, but it isn't the same thing at all. Actually there's nothing unfair in the natural distribution of merit. A real commitment to academic merit in this country would mean stopping the pretence that everyone can aspire to a university education, because it simply is not true; it is a harmful egalitarianism deception. (*ibid.*)

By failing to recognise how structural and institutional power shapes the selection of who will or will not have access to higher education, Marrin reaches a conclusion that re-establishes pre-existing hierarchies of power. She effectively re-authorises the delegitimisation of particular groups.

There are 'polarising discourses', in which students are constructed as normal or abnormal, worthy or unworthy, acceptable or unacceptable (Williams, 1997a: 25; Ball, 1990). Key 'icon' words are used, such as elite, standard and quality, and the unacceptability of their opposites is assumed: mass, non-standard, access (Williams, 1997a: 25).

> Meanings are constructed through explicit or more often implicit contrast; a positive rests upon the negative of something antithetical. The normal, the worthy student and the acceptable processes of admission are legitimised by references to the abnormal, the unworthy, the unacceptable. (*ibid.*: 26)

In light of how the constructs of 'class' and 'gender' reproduce binary thinking – for example that men are rational and women emotional, that middle-class culture is superior and working-class culture deficient – it is not surprising that many access students were afraid of being noticed in the classroom. Critical pedagogy seeks to 'give a voice' to students but this may well go against the desire of the students to remain silent and unnoticed. This desire for invisibility is shaped by historical, political and cultural contexts. Students do not want to be revealed as not belonging, not middle-class, and therefore, according to the embedded logic, not intelligent:

> *If it was someone like that fella who was very very intelligent then I'd be more quiet I think, because I wouldn't want him to think I was totally stupid in the questions that I ask. I mean I was listening to you for quite a while before I said anything. So I'd have to be listening for quite awhile before I'd actually say something.* (Amanda, 1999)

> *The first thing I was really frightened of was the speaking out.* (Linda, 1999)

Empowering education?

Access educators have attempted to 'empower' students through the practice of critical pedagogy in the access classroom (Anderson and Gardiner, 1998; McGivney, 1998; Maher and Tetreault, 1994; Macedo, 1994). Critical pedagogy has been seen as a tool for empowerment, leading to personal and social transformation and challenging the traditional hierarchical relationship between teacher and student (Morley, 1999: 101). The concept of empowerment comes to mean 'analysing ideas about the causes of powerlessness, recognising systematic oppressive forces, and acting both individually and collectively to change the conditions of our lives' (Lather, 1991: 4).

The empowerment project aims to 'give power' to the 'less powerful', which implies that tutors have power to distribute more equally to students. But power is not a possession and 'cannot be and is not distributed in the same way as, for example, slices of cake' (Epstein, 1993: 11). On the other hand, 'power can be and is distributed through the ways in which institutions...are organised and tends to accrue to certain groups of people – most obviously white, middle-class, heterosexual men' (*ibid.*).

Thus the concept of empowerment is highly contested. It has been critiqued by poststructural feminist academics (Gore, 1993; Luke and Gore, 1992; Lather, 1991), who point out that critical pedagogues are implicated in and perpetuate power inequalities, and so reflexivity is required to address such complicity. The concept of empowerment presupposes an agent of empowerment and places the feminist tutor in the superior position of rescuer and empowerer of 'others' (Morley, 1999: 105). Morley points out that 'this suggests that individuals or groups with more cultural capital, in terms of educational qualifications and professional status, can have power over those denied access to such capital' (*ibid.*: 111). She argues that:

> A postmodern view could articulate how...education is part of this manipulative network of power, in so far as it provides a constant surveillance of the individual and legitimates what counts as cultural capital. Empowerment can imply lack and a deviant passivity which must be worked on through new forms of disciplinary regimes such as watching, listening, knowing. (*ibid.*)

Empowerment becomes problematic when it assumes that tutors possess power over students, which creates new forms of disciplinary regimes. Empowerment is then merely another mechanism for marginalised groups to be observed, regulated, categorised and trained by those deemed to 'know better'.

Conscientisation or consciousness-raising is central to notions of empowerment in access education. This involves an awareness-raising process that leads to the students coming to recognise that their knowledge, experiences and ideas are highly valuable (Skeggs, 1997; Maher and Tetreault, 1994; Evans, 1995). The shift in self-perception and subjectivity, which also requires the shift in the way the 'other' is perceived, is potentially empowering. For example, Kerry explains a shift in her thinking from believing the tutors always to be right to realising that tutors have opinions which are of equal value to her own ideas and are not objective truths. She speaks about this in the context of a Sociology course, where she is arguing with the teacher that instincts and intuition do exist. He tells her she is wrong:

With this instinct thing, he came back with all these notes and – and I thought oh-oh, I can't do it [small laugh]. And uumm, I thought, well he thinks I'm wrong but these are my opinions, and I was speaking to my friend and she said, well Sociology is about different people's opinions, nobody says you're wrong, nobody says he's right. It's all about how you interpret different things. Just because you believe in things like intuition and he doesn't, doesn't mean that you're wrong. So once I got through that, I was able to say to the tutor, 'no, that's your opinion'. So that's a step forward for me, whereas before I would have thought that's it, I've finished now, I can't do it. (Kerry, 1999)

Kerry's account displays a significant shift in her subject positioning. The emphasis, though, is on *individual agency* rather than on the struggle to recognise, expose and transform *structural power relations*. Indeed, the empowerment project is itself constrained by the power relations that determine the subordinate position of the access student in relation to the middle-class lecturer. Access education for empowerment is always limited by wider social and structural relations. Access students are constrained by social and discursive dynamics, which reposition them according to age, class, dis/ability, gender and race relations. The dynamics are, however, made fluid through the agency of the subject and through shifting and contradictory discourses. The active subject may refuse or accept the positions available. Importantly, education provides a tool for *momentary* refusals and acceptances (Skeggs, 1997), a mechanism by which power relations may be temporarily contested and subject position boundaries provisionally remapped and redefined.

PB: *What is it you really love about science?*

Kerry: *Practical, I love doing it. It just stems from like opening presents, when you're a little girl and I used to just rip it up...you're doing something, I love hands on things. Like, I was brought up with my dad mending cars, and I could change a wheel when I was ten. It's hands on, always, you know I would tinker with car engines when I was little and I know how to change brake pads, because it's practical. And I'm a practical person. More so, than, uumm, an intel-*

lectual person, but I've built up that side of myself, that I can do the practical and the theory as well as each other.

Kerry accepts the subject position offered to her through the educational system; she is, she implies, inherently practical and not intellectual; those characteristics associated with being working class. However, she actively re-frames her position by arguing that she is able to build up the other side of herself: the intellectual. It may not be 'natural' to her but she can do theory, and therefore middle-class identity. She connects her practical skill with her ability to understand science, redefining the practical as a necessary and valuable skill in accessing certain forms of (middle class) knowledge. Finally, she challenges gender stereotypes by naturalising the ability of girls to do things like change brake pads and understand and enjoy science. She actively re-maps her social position across the boundaries of gender and class.

However such agency is fragile and too easily undermined in the access classroom. Charity illustrates this point when she describes her frustration over students' contributions being *listened* to but not *heard* as serious ideas:

> I think if the development of ideas starts to happen there's umm, there's a sense of ideas not being valued for what they are: **ideas**. There's a sense of: 'oh yes, well I see that, but actually this is what's important'. So it's almost a sort of umm, you know, there might be some kind of listening, but not actually a developing of [students' ideas] you know? (Charity, 1999)

Intimidating exams

The undermining of students can also take place during assessments.

> If I pass my Psychology exam that will be a bonus. (Vanessa, 1999)

> I'm quite happy learning, just learning about it and if I do pass then that's a bonus. So that's my perspective on it. (Linda, 1999)

Many participants claimed that they did not expect to pass exams but that it would be a bonus if they did. It seemed that access students are motivated purely by the learning process and attribute little significance to grades and qualifications. But this attitude could also be a defence mechanism, a way for students to protect themselves from the shame of 'failure'. Non-traditional students actively protect themselves against the disappointment of being labelled 'academically unworthy', an identity that many have carried with them since their early schooling.

The examination system is generally accepted as an objective exercise that reveals the 'true' position of a student against the declared measure of excellence and failure and against the other students s/he is competing with. Foucault argues that the examination is an instrument of 'disciplinary power' (Foucault, 1975). Its success derives 'from the use of simple instruments: hierarchical observation, normalising judgement, and their combination in a procedure that is specific to it – the examination' (Foucault, 1984: 188). The exercise of disciplinary power:

> presupposes a mechanism that coerces by means of observation;
> an apparatus in which the techniques that make it possible to see
> induce effects of power and in which, conversely, the means of
> coercion make those on whom they are applied clearly visible.
> (*ibid.*: 189)

In the examination, the lay-out of the exam room is crucial to the observation of students: 'the spatial 'nesting' of hierarchized surveillance' (*ibid.*: 190). This includes, for example, the architecture of the college, the distance between desks, and the invigilator who watches carefully over the examinees. Through the 'normalising judgement' exercised in the examination process, each individual is given a mark of distinction and differentiated from all the others by means of 'an average to be respected, an optimum toward which one must move' (*ibid.*: 195). The examination operates as a mechanism of surveillance. It creates the possibility to qualify, classify and to exclude:

> The examination transformed the economy of visibility into the exer-
> cise of power. And the examination is the technique by which
> power, instead of emitting signs of its potency, instead of imposing
> its mark on its subjects, holds them in a mechanism of objectifica-
> tion. In this space of domination disciplinary power manifests the

potency essentially by arranging objects. The examination is, as it were, the ceremony of this objectification. (Foucault, 1975: 187)

Through this system, judgements are made about who the student is, what s/he is capable of and her/his social position. It introduces the binary opposite of 'good and bad', by placing the student on a continuum with the 'best' at one end and the 'worst' at the other (Canaan, 1997: 172). It is a system that access students remember well from school and they understand it as objective and fair because the examination system has shaped their self-perceptions and self-expectations since childhood.

> *Luckily enough me Mum and Dad never ever were like some parents, cause they knew I weren't really academically that bright and at least I didn't have the pressure from them keeping pushing me and telling me do this, telling me to do that. I never had any of that, so I was grateful I suppose for that. But then when I went into Secondary School umm yes I was put, yes it was a band system then, and I think that it went A, B and C or it was A and B were the top and I was right at the bottom. You had top middle and bottom and I was always at the bottom anyway. I still didn't really do very good in that at all. Looking back, I don't really think they were that helpful. As I say they just dismissed you as if you were really thick and that's it; they concentrate on the ones that could do it. (Amanda, 1999)*

> *And the 11 plus system was in at the primary school. And I don't remember any discussions or knowledge or anything being taught about the fact that we were going to have this examination. There was no preparation whatsoever. I can remember suddenly getting wind that this was going to happen and then panicking, literally feeling quite panicked about what was going on and what was going to be expected. Anyway, I went ahead and we sat this exam and I don't know who got through and who didn't all I know is that I obviously failed... but it was almost like there was this expectation that certain people wouldn't get through. (Charity, 1999)*

Grades are seen as reflections of individual value and reinforce cultural myths about fairness and meritocracy. The students fear that getting poor grades will prove that they are naturally unintelligent and will justify their subordinate social position. The construction of working-class identity as inferior has the potential to be re-affirmed through the examination process.

There is therefore real tension between the ethos of access education and the examination system. Cheryl Law argues that 'assessment needs to consider the nature of the knowledge involved' (1998: 63). Access education is at odds with a system that is based on assumptions about the validity of standardised assessment methods as universal measurements of student worth. Not only does the examination serve as a reinforcement of inequalities between those who have the 'right' cultural capital and those who do not, but it also serves to undermine the access tutor by her/his location in the academy. My colleague explained her serious reservations about the use of examinations in access education:

> *Christine told me how intelligent her students were, but many of them had dyslexia which held them back. She said with the emphasis on examinations they just could not get through, no matter how intelligent they were.* (Research diary, 15 June, 1999)

Canaan expresses her personal concerns about the examination process:

> When I grade students' essays, I am most fully enacting my position as power-knowledge broker, locating my students at discrete places along a hierarchically ranked continuum which is thought to indicate their worth as students. (Cannan, 1997: 173)

Sadie speaks in detail about her fear of exams − a fear that has not dissipated during three years of educational participation. She highlights the intimidating way that exams serve to reposition students in terms of their social value, and the repercussions they have on their future decisions, choices and opportunities. Such regulating mechanisms feed back to the ways that individuals perceive themselves and their future prospects:

> Sadie: *Until I get to the day when I'm sitting there doing the exam I'll be, I'll be worrying about it. But it's only because I'm so terrible at exams that I worry about them. It's just the worry − you can't stop yourself. That's the way you are about exams − you worry about*

*them. You worry about them. You're never right as well. If you could
do it, if you weren't stressed about the thought that you've come to
the exam – I've got to do my best –*

PB: *Yeah...do you think exams are unfair?*

Sadie: *Yeah, I do a bit. I think because there's so much percentage
on them, and I think there should be more on how well you've done
in the year, how well you've done in coursework. That's really how
well you do as a student. I do think they are unfair. Some people just
get on with them and don't pain over them, but they do let you
down. They do let you down. Which is why I try to do my best in my
coursework, try to make up my grade... I know, even if I revised
every day from now to my exams, I wouldn't do any better than if I
left it to a couple of months before, because I blank anyway when I
get in there. It does gradually come back, but then you've run out of
time. And your writing's all messy and you've got spelling mistakes
and... things like that. It's awful. I hate them. I know you've got to
have them, but I don't think they show who you really are. You can
end up getting a grade you don't deserve. There'd be a lot more
people out there doing well in education and moving on, but they
just don't get recognised in exams. And then they feel 'gawd, I must
be awful' but they're not really. You just panic too much. And that's
what I'm dreading, that I'll know in myself if I don't do that well, I'll
know it's not me.*

Sadie's talk weaves in and out of various vantage points: she moves
between 'I', 'you', 'they' in a way that captures students' sense of
powerlessness over achievement in a system that places greatest
emphasis on the 'objective' examination. Although she claims that
'you can end up getting a grade you don't deserve', she also explains
that exam results directly affect future opportunities and students'
ability 'to move on'. Her switch from 'I' to 'they' indicates her frustration and fear that ultimately she does not have control over the
examination process in the same way as she feels she has control of
the *learning* process. It is ultimately examinations, not herself, that
will let her down.

Although access teachers are constrained by their location in the
formal educational institution, and the student is the object of

'normalising judgements', the story is not entirely pessimistic. Access education is a site of struggle and possible change (Morley, 1999: 99). Its ideologies penetrate educational spaces, providing opportunities for resistance. Students may actively reject the examination's objectifying process, refusing to accept its values and judgements. Although students may not always leave their courses as 'winners' or as 'success stories', they may leave with a re-defined notion of the academic world and reject the objective claims it makes and the subject positions it proposes to and imposes on students. This extract illustrates these issues:

> John: *I think I've decided that I don't belong at university.*
>
> PB: *Why, why do you feel that way?*
>
> John: *Why do I feel that way? Good question! Um, because I'm not so sure how much I agree with it for starters and I'm not – I don't know how I would respond to being there, that environment; it's just the whole emphasis. It's how you measure intelligence at the end of the day. For me it's not particularly somebody's um, intellectual ability; it's just that whole idea how, um, what value our society has towards intellectual greatness and to me it's a double-edged sword really. Cause it could also be the great failure of our society.*

And later he adds:

> *[Access to Higher Education] gave me an injection of confidence on one level to be – to be me a bit more. You know, uh, I mean I don't feel intimidated or anything like that. I don't feel intimidated anymore by the whole idea of uh university and the wonders of university.*
>
> PB: *Is that one of the reasons you feel you don't need to do it now maybe?*
>
> John: *Possibly... Yeah. But, I'm not 100% sure if I don't want to do it, you know, but at the moment I don't feel there's a place for me there. I mean it could all be so different.*
>
> PB: *How could it all be different?*
>
> John: *How could it all be different? Gosh!*
>
> PB: *Yeah, I mean tell me, ideally what would it be like?*

John: *What we need is the whole way education and the whole system to be completely redefined and um, from the very first, you know, tentative steps. I mean I'm speaking of adult education. The whole criteria...I don't know where to start. History should be about all cultures, and we do need to learn about British history but we need to learn about the negative effects of colonialism and all stuff like that. We need to incorporate the whole in every subject, everybody's point of view. Students need to have an opportunity to express their views and whatever their views are they need to be expressed and considered valid. Because people go to classes and immediately they feel inferior because they don't understand something. Which is a ridiculous situation, because what they are being taught anyway isn't necessarily the way things are anyway, and if they don't understand it there's no reason they should be made to feel inferior. To me education should be like a healing process, an exploration through knowledge of the world, and an exploration of the world. There's space and scope for everybody. Everyone is considered.*

John's insights offer a framework for those committed to widening participation. His comments highlight the student position within the complex web of institutional power and the limits and possibilities for social transformation that students face. He reminds us of the structural and discursive factors which continue to influence students' experiences and the institutional barriers to equality and justice.

The accounts and critiques of students provide a rich insight into the problems facing access education and identify crucial issues about effectively widening participation. Challenging the organisation and content of the curriculum and the politics of the academy is one key area. Continually re-evaluating and reflexively examining our pedagogical approaches in the classroom is another. It is also important to question assumptions about objectivity in standardised assessment.

The next chapter considers the impact of multiple and contradictory discourses on the lives and experiences of access students. Many of those who return to education are on a journey of self-discovery.

Although education may provide liberating spaces for marginalised groups, it also causes uncertainties and confusions as the students precariously negotiate their shifting subjectivities.

6
Reconstructing the Self through Educational Participation

Upon proof-reading this essay, it seems to finish in mid-sentence. I feel it reflects 'where I am' at the moment. I know that I will be able to keep adding to it as I start to choose the directions I take instead of being led by circumstances. (Greg, coursework: A Self-Reflective Essay, 1999)

There is nothing wrong with change as long as it's for the best? Unfortunately this statement reflects only those who believe the best is for them. Those around us may have a different point of view. What we do have to consider is the consequences of each change. Are we prepared to take the chances and if so have any of us thought about the end result? (Vanessa, coursework: Changes, April 1998)

Introduction

This chapter examines the participants' desire for self-discovery. According to poststructural thought:

> the fully unified, completed secure and coherent identity is a fantasy. Instead, as the systems of meaning and cultural representation multiply, we are confronted by a bewildering, fleeting multiplicity of possible identities, any one of which we could identify with – at least temporarily. (Hall, 1992: 227)

Identity formation, a complex interaction between inner and outer worlds, is a destabilising process of 'becoming' rather than 'being'. This complex interaction is represented through the concept 'subjectivity'. This chapter explores how participants construct their subjectivity in relation to the multiple contexts in which they are positioned and position themselves. It is concerned with the complexity and diversity of gender and the ways people 'are both 'made subject' by/within the social order and how they are agents/subjects within/against it' (Jones, 1993: 158). Subjects occupy multiple, changing and contradictory positions through shifting discourses.

> The subject of poststructuralism, unlike the humanist subject, then is constantly in process; it only exists as process; it is revised and (re)presented through images, metaphors, storylines and other features of language, such as pronoun grammar; it is spoken and respoken, each speaking existing in a palimpsest[1] with others. (Davies, 1997: 275)

Education, although associated with self-discovery, intensifies the project of 'becoming' as an uncertain and unstable process. Four related analytical tools helped examine the participants' shifting subjectivities: the **positioned discourse** and the **shifting positions discourse** (Mauthner and Hey, 1999: 79), the concept of **identification** (Hall, 1992:287) and the concept of **positionality** (Alcoff, 1988).

Of the four discourses Melanie Mauthner formulates in her research on sister relationships, two are useful for this chapter; the positioned discourse and the shifting positions discourse (Mauthner and Hey, 1999; Mauthner, 1998a). She describes them as 'analytical tools for conceptualising power relations and changing subjectivity' (ibid.). They are useful for thinking about the dynamics of subjectivity and access students' relationship to education. The participants reveal the struggle involved as subjectivity changes through education and the tensions created between the production of self as fixed and the production of self as becoming.

Stuart Hall makes a distinction between 'identity' and 'identification', which captures the difference between imagining ourselves as 'being' rather than in the process of 'becoming'.

> Thus, rather than speaking of identity as a finished thing, we should speak of *identification*, and see it as an on-going process. Identity arises, not so much from the fullness of identity which is already inside us as individuals, but from a *lack* of wholeness which is 'filled' from *outside* us, by the ways we imagine ourselves to be seen by *others*. Psychoanalytically, the reason why we continually search for 'identity', constructing biographies which knit together the different parts of our divided selves into a unity, is to recapture this fantasised pleasure of fullness (plenitude). (Hall, 1992: 287-8, original emphases)

Many access students find their way back to education because of their longing for a clearly defined self-identity. In our common-sense understanding, identity is perceived as fixed, individual, stable and unique. Well-used British expressions such as 'just be yourself' reinforce such Western understandings of what it means to be an individual. However, identity formation is far more complex than this, connected as it is to a complex web of social relations, structures and discourses. Who we are on the inside is linked to the outer world. This chapter maps the ways the participants come to identify themselves with multiple and contradictory positions within the nexus of social, cultural, economic and discursive relations. Identity is fluid and changing, and possibilities for new identifications are forged through social change but, at the same time, identity is fixed in the sense that social structures reproduce people through systemic inequities such as class, gender and 'race'. Although structural inequalities may have altered, new forms of classism, neo-colonialism, racism and sexism constrain our journey through and against different subject positions (such as the subject position 'student', for example).

Positionality throws light on how participants occupy multiple subject positions while also perceiving themselves as fixed and stable. Becoming a learner intensifies these contradictory sensibilities of the self as fixed, against a subjectivity that is radical[2], multiple, complex and ever changing. An examination of these contradictory sensibilities reveals the interrelationship between subjectivity and experience.

We see how the participants represent themselves as autonomous individuals with a fixed and stable identity (for example English, working-class woman), while experiencing self-transformation through educational participation. What does this mean for their experiences as wives, mothers, daughters, sons, manual labourers, and so on? How does education operate as a catalyst for recognising shifting identities? Is education experienced as only a positive influence in their lives and relationships or is this part of the access education rhetoric? Is access education ever experienced as disruptive and contradictory or is it always experienced as progressive? How might access students challenge oppressive discourses and take up radical subject positions?

Education as a search for self

And, you know, I'd had Lewis, I had two children, I thought no, I don't want any more. I had to find something for myself. I knew there was a me there. I'd done my bit as a mum. Now I had to go back and find a me. (Vanessa, 1999)

The participants described education as a journey of self-discovery. Their desire to 'find a me' assumes an essential, autonomous, pre-discursive self; a self with 'untapped potential':

PB: *What happened to make you think about returning to education?*

Charity: *When I left secondary and went into the offices, I very quickly realised that, you know, I had all this potential that wasn't being utilised...*

The idea of a self with untapped potential draws on a neo-liberal discourse, which positions access students as 'deserving returners': individuals with 'talent and merit which could and should be given the opportunity to be developed' (Green and Webb, 1997: 138). This discourse implies an essential self that either has *natural* academic ability or does not. The speech made by John Randall, the Chief Executive of the Quality Assurance Agency for Higher Education for the QAA Recognition Scheme for Access, on 11 March 1999 characterised this discourse:

John Randall started his speech with the words: 'Access matters because standards matter' and expressed his great support for the movement to widen educational participation. However he then expressed his great concern that 'individuals who would not benefit from higher education should not be recruited to Access programmes, because this would mean setting them up for failure, and thereby creating bad role models for their children'. (Research Diary, 11 March 1999)

This discourse ignores the way that selectivity operates through admissions policies to reinforce social differentiation. Admissions are based on fixed categories that contain cultural and historical meanings associated with, for example, class, gender, nationality and race (Williams, 1997c: 159). Through discourses of selectivity, participants are identified and identify themselves as deserving or undeserving, legitimate or illegitimate, in terms of the categories of 'standard' and 'non-standard', 'traditional' and 'non-traditional'. Access students who apply for university places are positioned as 'non-standard' in comparison with the perceived opposite; the 'normal' 'A' level student aged 18 (Webb, 1997: 68). Moreover, access students adopt categories that become familiar to them through the discursive practices of admissions tutors. 'Such practices have legitimised the divisions between students using the categories of age, gender, 'race' and class as well as types of qualifications' (*ibid.*: 151).

Nevertheless, it is through neo-liberal discourse that the 'non-standard' student can be rescued to become 'deserving' and 'legitimate' but only when they are deemed as containing 'untapped potential'. Categories such as 'non-standard' simultaneously and contradictorily reposition students as 'worthy' or 'unworthy' according to their positionality and qualifications. Thus, the availability of the neo-liberal discourse of the 'deserving student with untapped potential' enables some subjects (those seen to possess academic potential) to reconsider the identity of learner. What is written out of the discourse is how certain subjects become positioned as having potential while others do not.

This neo-liberal discourse constructs education as a project which is essentially about individual and social progress. The notion of individual progress presupposes a unitary and continuous self. Social progress is a key aim of modernity. It is through education that individual and social progress might be achieved, as students are taught the power of science, objectivity and positivism as the route to enlightenment through logic and reason (Lather, 1991: 5).

During conversations, both the participants and I continually reproduced this idea that education is centrally about progress:

> Kerry: *And I think he thought you know you need to be home because of the children and why do you feel the need to go to college and my answer was I want to better myself...Which is what people do isn't it, why they go to college?*
>
> PB: *Yeah*

However, poststructural theory makes the notion of progress problematic (Lather, 1991; Usher, 1997). Progress itself is only a discourse rather than the ultimate truth to be reached through scientific reason, because meanings around progress are not fixed and universally shared. What may represent progress to an eugenicist, for example, may be very different from what would be seen as progress by a socialist feminist or an access tutor. Hegemonic discourses of individual progress contain narratives about 'success' – measured in terms of competition with other individuals within a social hierarchical framework. The common-sense link between widening educational participation, individual progress and success is encapsulated in the title *Learning to Succeed* (June 1999) of the government white paper on lifelong learning. The project of 'success' is always understood as positive and desirable within dominant discourses, despite the anguish and pain often caused by the drive for success (Lucey, 2000). Moreover, participants' accounts reveal that education does not *only* represent instrumental oriented meanings around progress and success. It also represents, among other things, a space for self.

Mapping out a space for self through educational participation

An historical examination of women's autobiographies documents their strategic use of education to resist 'the space restrictions imposed upon their lives' and to try to create 'new space boundaries for themselves... beyond masculinist geographical closures' (Tamboukou, 1999:127). Longing for a 'space for self' is a recurring theme in the female participants' narratives.

> *I've not done this for anybody else. I've done this for me.* (Linda, 1999)

> *And [college] was for me, because I found it so fascinating anyway... I just want to go because I like being there.* (Vanessa, 1999)

Women's struggle for space has a long history, as eloquently argued by Virginia Woolf in her essay *A Room of One's Own*, first published in 1929. Although gender structures have changed, women continue to be constructed through discourses of femininity as naturally selfless, while men are perceived as innately self-oriented through hegemonic masculinity. Such characterisations continue to be heightened through motherhood (Nicolson, 1997; Pascall and Cox, 1993: 62). As Britton and Baxter (1999: 190) explain:

> For women to prioritise their own needs is to challenge both the cultural assumptions about women's place and the patriarchal domestic division of labour.

It is now acceptable for women to demand time and space for themselves, but this is usually measured against the ability to fulfil and prioritise their role as 'good mothers' first – whether or not they are mothers (Lawrence, 1987: 214). Interestingly, participants with children continually revealed feelings of guilt in relationship to their learning, seen as a deviant activity stealing their time and energies away from their rightful responsibilities.

> *I must admit I did feel guilty for going, whenever I, when I got to college, when I was actually in the classroom it felt good, it felt really nice... I did feel guilty for going... I felt guilty because it was something I was doing for myself, when I felt I should have been at home, even though Luke was like at nursery school.* (Vanessa)

Valerie Hey examines forms of 'emotional restructuring' within education and argues that 'one form of emotional readjustment is shaped through the mobilisation and amplification of female guilt' (Hey, 1996: 356). The lifelong learning discourse mobilises female guilt by pointing up the responsibility of 'good parents' to take up lifelong learning opportunities in order to help their children achieve at school. There are certainly real benefits for many women and their children in participating in learning. However, the common-sense leap to the notion that 'helping themselves' is *primarily* about 'helping their children' should be contested. Part of the contemporary 'good parent' discourse includes the responsibility (for mothers) to improve the opportunities of their children by strategically and actively planning upward social mobility by gaining qualifications. This generates yet another pressure for mothers to prove their success. Such responsibility is embedded in the neo-liberal narrative about competitive individuals who, in a society seen as classless, capitalise on equally available opportunities to provide the 'best' life possible for their children. All this is seen to be achievable through lifelong learning programmes, which are themselves understood as universally available and accessible. Class, disability, gender, ethnicity, sexuality and 'race' are written out of the discourse. Gaining educational access becomes a parental *responsibility* as well as, or even over and above, an individual right. 'Parental responsibility' is presented as an 'ungendered concept' (Standing, 1999), and families are positioned as individual autonomous units, expected to exercise both their citizen's rights and responsibilities and contribute to, rather than drain, national stability and competitiveness (Giddens, 1998: 94-8). The discourse ignores all differences between and within families.

Discourses of educational participation and lifelong learning

Labour policies of lifelong learning require all 'citizens' to compete in a rapidly changing employment market by gaining new skills and qualifications (DfEE, June 1999). Citizens have the right to educational access *because of* their responsibility to adapt to change by updating their skills according to the needs of national and global economies. Education becomes collapsed into a national training project to regenerate the economy. Yet such policy presents the notion of citizenship as an 'unproblematic, ungendered concept, free from class and cultural associations' (Standing, 1999: 57).

Against the discourse of policy texts, the participants do not explain learning as primarily about parental and/or citizen responsibilities. John, when he describes his choice to return to education, challenges the dominant discourses of widening participation:

> John: *I was disillusioned with school and my aspiration was I wanted to – to find happiness inside.*
>
> PB: *Did you have any idea how you were going to do that?*
>
> John: *I had no idea about how I was going to go about it. All I knew was that at 16 I had to leave school and I had to go and get a job. I just had a thirst for something but I didn't know what it was. And because of that I just fell into jobs, people that I knew, so it was all like that, all my working life it's been like that... My first thought about returning to education – I think I was about 20, by which time, my little inner quest turned its self outwards into the fight for, you know, social justice, and I was raging for this. And I thought I must go back to education so I applied to an Access course when I was 22 and – against my better judgement I'd say actually. They were oversubscribed so fortunately I didn't get in. Instinctively I knew it wasn't the right thing to do. I really did. Because I was very very weary of you know, not necessarily the educational system, but the intellectual – the whole intellectual mindset thing, you know. I didn't want to get involved in it, because I knew I would just become even more frustrated and even more chewed up inside. So fortunately I didn't get in.*

John then spent two years working with his father in the factory, which he described as 'terrible and fantastic', because 'it grounded [him] and surrounded [him] with lots of people with lots of problems'. He was then unemployed for two years, which he describes as 'quite a revelation to me':

> John: *It was quite a positive process, you know, being out of the system in that way, and being so isolated and...you know when all*

the alienation and everything is gone, when I stopped making a comparison with me and everyone else and how I didn't fit in...when that process stopped it began to be a wonderful process, like almost a healing process. It gave me time and room to breathe at last after all this time.

After two years of unemployment, his brother offered him a job where he has stayed for six years. When I asked what brought him back to the Access course, he explains:

John: *Well, there was something that was still undone in my mind about, uh, the intelligentsia if you like. And I needed to settle it and to make a decision once and for all. The other reason was, you know, the nature of the work my brother and I do...it's very very demanding. I've got an injury on my knee because of it, and I've got an injury on my heart because of it and basically my body is not coping with it anymore and the time is right to try again. I mean, I guess it was really to do with the position with the job, I was exhausted and my body was broken and I knew that in a sense that this was my final option, you know, so that's why I pursued it I guess. I mean if I was healthy and fit maybe I wouldn't have but because I wasn't I did.*

John's educational experiences and 'choices' are shaped by his positionality as a white, working-class male. His understandings about his identity and experiences of learning, work and relationships are formed by his subjectivity, which leads him to question the dominant neo-liberal discourses surrounding him that fail to connect with his lived and material reality. His narrative demonstrates the ability of the subject to actively make meaning against dominant modes of thinking. It also reveals a search for space free of surveillance, which he discovers briefly through a period of unemployment, a space that enables him to contest and redefine social and personal meanings. John's story demonstrates simultaneously the material constraints imposed by structures of class and gender and the limitations of being positioned as a working-class male. Although he struggles against these oppressive factors, his material existence continues to be influenced by them, because, for example, he has no other 'choice' but to take the hard physical work available to him as a working-class man (Connell, 1995: 55; Willis, 1977). Connell's concept of 'body reflexive practices' sheds light on the constraints and control available to John in relation to his sense of self (Connell, 1995). For example, the subject position of manual labourer profoundly affects his body and ultimately leads to his decision to return to education. Yet his new position as student is contradictory to dominant versions of white working-class masculinity tied to physical labour. His educational participation did not represent a quest for success or assuming responsibility as a 'good citizen'. It represented a hope and longing for emancipatory spaces, inner happiness and social justice.

John came to education as a final 'choice' after suffering physically from the kinds of material and emotional pressures associated with working class masculinity. The discourses available to him and the experiential aspects of these are social, culminating in gendered and classed oppressions. Yet these discourses and experiences also made available to him the subjectivity of learner, active agent and critical knower.

Deconstruction of my representations reveals my own desire for continuity and for an understanding of education as progressive. Education is seen through our accounts as something that is always 'good' for people. However, a poststructural reading of our accounts exposes the pain, as well as the pleasure, the contradiction as well as the continuity, the confusion as well as the clarity, with which education is experienced. This is now explored.

The reconstruction of different separate 'me's'

Participants recognise themselves as multiply positioned (e.g. as wife, mother, student, friend, carer, brother, daughter, worker and so forth) and experience the contradictions between and within these multiple identities. A tendency seems to be to divide these neatly up into private/public selves, drawing on a patriarchal discourse. The different strands of self are seen as separate and compatible, rather than as overlapping, conflicting, contradictory and discontinuous. This is embedded in the binary gender construction of the caring self-sacrificial mother and the autonomous self-oriented worker.

PB: *How have you managed learning and your other respon-sibilities at the same time? Learning and your work and your work at home as a – as a mother...*

Vicky: *It's a role. It's really strange 'cause every part of life is a role. You act a role, don't you. You go to college, you do your work. You study. You come home, you are the mum, you cook the dinner, you do the ironing. And I go to the gym – I'm a different person. I cope really well. And I've sectioned every part off... it's really strange, but if I want to go out with my friends, have a great time and a laugh and a drink, that is me... the single me whose having – got no responsibilities and I enjoy myself. When I'm the wife and the mum I'm at home and here for them.*

However Vicky's strategy to divide herself up into separate 'me's' is partially a reaction to the policing of her sexuality and gender re/positioning that is taking place in her home. She describes how her husband and nineteen year-old son question her whenever she leaves the house:

Vicky: *Now I'm like neglecting [my husband] a bit and I want to go out with the girls now and again and have some fun clubbing and do my work, and I have quite a responsible job where I work and... he's like, before I go out he might turn around and say 'where have you been'... 'how long have you been'...'where are you going' and it's just – too much. Sunday was an example...my husband was working and my eldest son come downstairs about 11 o'clock and I was going out and he said 'where you going'. And I really didn't want to tell him where I was going, it was private to me where I was going. So he said 'where are you going' and I said 'I'm not telling you where I'm going' and he said 'why, have you got something to hide?' And I just walked out and thought 'I don't need this and I don't have to tell everyone where I'm going!'*

It seems that the *shifting position* discourse available to working-class women through access education may cause complex tensions, dilemmas and struggles for their *positioned discourse* within the family. Although an aim of access education is to disrupt the oppressions located within positioned discourse, the process of negotiating a way through changing and contradictory subjectivities may be a painful one.

Vicky: *How can I put it... in a way... it's... now I'm doing what I want to do, I feel as though certain people are watching me and it's suffocating me... the suffocation frightens me.*

As the participants struggle to discover new space for self, 'somewhere to retreat... somewhere beyond control, beyond surveillance' (Tamboukou, 1999: 133), the space they occupy in the domestic sphere becomes more heavily policed by others. As Tamboukou argues, 'space is fundamental in any exercise of power':

> Home seems to operate as a 'panopticon', Bentham's architectural device, which for Foucault represents the triumph of disciplinary technology (Foucault, 1991, pp. 195-228). In such conditions of permanent visibility, women seem to be always watched, to the smallest detail of their activities. Home is therefore turned to a locale where even if there are discontinuities and dispersion in the gaze of the other, women's integral surveillance is being carried on. (Tamboukou, 1999: 132)

Classed and gendered subjectivities

The search for self is classed, gendered, racialised and sexualised. For example, Vanessa positions herself in relation to her husband and children through the discourse of class and gender:

PB: *What did [your husband] think?*

Vanessa: *That I was just gonna be really brainy and not want him – not want him and the kids and I'd want a different life altogether and go be with all these really intellectual people.*

Her talk, in relationship to her family, plays with the idea of a 'brainy' self, drawing on positioned discourses of class and gender:

Vanessa: *Well it's someone training for a job isn't it – umm – he'd have to try and – for me that's what it was – you know I'm training myself up to be something different – NOT like I say to be extremely intellectual because I'm not, it's just I've got some brains there and I want to use them and I never have done in the past and now, I suppose at my time of life, I feel it's what I want to do – and the kids see it as well, I mean uh I don't know if them loving school like they do is anything to do with me you know getting up in the*

109

mornings and going to college and stuff like that. Maybe it is, but they see me doing my work and 'cause Carley will be going to Juniors in September and she says 'oh you get homework with that!' and maybe me bringing my homework home and she sees Mummy doing it it'll give her an incentive and Rick started saying things like 'oh, I think she'll end up going to University' and I say 'no I don't think she's that way inclined – she'll probably go to college, because she's quite intellectual herself' but umm, but yeah, it was difficult there were a lot of times that I gave up...

Vanessa continually reminds us that she is at college to train for work, not to go to university. She carefully selected the word 'training' over 'education' to signify her classed position, refusing the production of an intellectual self through learning. She then highlights the relationship between studenthood and motherhood, justifying her educational participation by reference to her parental responsibilities. She is regulating the reproduction of her subjectivity as a working-class mother. To reconstruct herself as 'too brainy' would threaten her position as wife of a working-class man. She avoids confrontation with the contradictions she experiences as she weaves her way precariously through access education while trying to maintain her position as wife and mother.

Marie is far more explicit about tensions between a sense of her self as fixed through class and her shifting subjectivity through education:

PB: *Are there any other obstacles you can think of in terms of your ability to benefit from education?*

Marie: *Well, I think that the class thing as well comes into it. Even though I feel quite confident, I still go into situations where I feel, you know, people are not like me. So I suppose that's part of it. And just that – just that no one else has those expectations of me...it's not expected that I achieve anything... my family [her parents and sister] are just... you know whereas if they were sort of saying – if they were encouraging or even questioning, you'd think 'oh I must get on with it' but it's not as though I even think 'oh because they don't care I've got to achieve something – I've got to do it' because it's just irrelevant to them so it's just you know...nothing.*

Marie imagines what it would mean to be positioned as the daughter of middle class parents, signified by her pronoun choice: '*you'd* think 'oh, I must get on with it'. Her parents' working-class position is central to her identity. As she engages with the middle-class discourses of the academy and the nursing profession, she is positioned as an outsider: 'People are not like me'.

Constructing the outsider: otherness and difference

Marie fantasises about fitting in to educational and medical sites through middle-class positionality. Otherness and difference are areas of identity that shape participants' experiences as access students. At one point Marie rejects the subject position 'student':

> PB: *What was it like to be part of a group of students?*

> Marie: *[long pause] I don't identify myself as a student! [she laughs] When you say that – I think of the women in that group – I suppose we were students...but I just think of us as a group of women and friends and people I'd made acquaintances with – I wouldn't look at us as a group of students. That might sound mad but that's how I felt. It was more like people who were doing the same thing as me, you know they didn't become close friends but they were friends and people to talk to.*

Yet at other times she describes herself as a student:

> *As a mature student it's easier, because of the way you're treated by the tutors and its your responsibility, and you know if you want to do it you can, if you don't want you don't have to. But it's harder to achieve in other ways – family life, commitments. It's an alien environment to me.*

Although she identifies as a student, she positions herself as different through the category 'mature student'. She describes herself as occupying an 'alien environment' when she attends the College and positions herself as 'not fitting in' as a student at the College.

Fitting in – or not – was a common theme in the participants' accounts. They often described schooling as centring on the attempt to fit in with peers, contrasting this to not needing to fit in at the College. This was a particularly significant concern throughout Sadie's narrative of educational participation. The transition from not fitting in at secondary school, due to 'physically not belonging', to fitting in with the popular girls after she had gained weight to 'get' a boyfriend, transformed her experience of schooling from dread to pleasure. Having a boyfriend meant that she 'felt like one of them'. She relaxed in her lessons and for the first time spoke in class, because *before* she 'didn't want to be seen'. Her decision to leave the sixth form was influenced by the absence of the 'popular girls'. At work she felt 'totally out of place' because the other employees were older women. In her other jobs, she perceived herself as incompetent, although her bosses seemed to think she was 'fine'. Her identity as incompetent was constructed through her continual comparison of herself with 'the other women' where she worked, who were 'really confident' and 'could laugh when they made mistakes'. Comparing work to school, she felt she was always being watched and says

> *If someone watches me, my mind goes blank. I thought 'I'm terrible at everything'.*

Sadie stopped working, stayed in her bedroom and isolated herself, fantasising about death. It was through such despair that her doctor, a woman whom she regards as a lifelong ally, suggested she take a course at the College. She enrolled on two GCSE courses, which she represents as entirely different from school:

> *The tutors were more relaxed and it was your choice to come to college. You were not put on the spot, not shouted at. I didn't exactly fit in, but that didn't matter much. I am happier now in my A level class because I fit in more with everyone else.*

Sadie's identification as a learner has often collided with her identification as '(not) fitting in'. Her identity is both fluid and positional in relation to the other subjects she interacts with. Feminist poststructural theory provides a framework, then, for thinking about change through the sites of subjectivity and education.

Educational space for constructing radical subjectivities

How might access education provide opportunities for students to deconstruct their subjectivities and refashion radical subjectivities?

The question forms the focus of this final section. Subjectivity is central to a politics of social justice because it is through subjectivity that hegemonic discourses are reproduced. It is also through subjectivity that discourses might be radically challenged and transformed. As Mrs Jones explains:

> *Imagine like, I don't know, like I'm a seed, and I have been planted into the soil. Well two years ago, I was still in the soil. Now, like two years on I'm like the shoot. So umm really within the next year or two I might be the flower. But I've just got to build up slowly. So I can't, I would really like to do Law, it does really interest me, but umm, at the moment I'm not strong enough to say I'll do Law, just not confident yet, but I'll get there. I know I will.*

The metaphor Mrs Jones uses here of herself as a seed conjures images of an essential self that develops in a progressive and predictable way, slowly reaching towards the ultimate point of growth as the flower. It draws on notions of individual progress discussed earlier in the chapter. However, she also represents herself as changing and in process. The self-image she creates is of female strength and creativity, resonate of radical feminist discourses.

Similarly, both dominant and radical discourses construct Vicky's understanding of her changing subjectivity:

> PB: *Umm, what about your self-identity, how has that changed... how you see yourself?*

> Vicky: *Oh, very much so – changed. Um, I see myself as a very positive person, a lot of the time, obviously everyone gets down. But I feel confident within myself – ready to face the world* [small laugh]. *Now I'd say no, umm, I see myself as an individual now,* [rather than a wife and mother] *who works, earns good money, goes shopping when I want to...*

Clearly, Vicky's changing sense of self is not only constituted from radical discourses. Her description fits with neo-liberal discourses constructing subjects as employees and consumers. But she also draws on liberal feminist discourses. Her role as wife and mother is secondary to her identity as an independent individual with her own needs.

There is a problem with change through education that stretches no further than the subject's own sense of individuality. This fails to challenge hegemonic discourses that reproduce social inequalities and mechanisms of oppression. Although both Mrs Jones and Vicky represent themselves as becoming more liberated women, they understand such change and remain positioned within neo-liberal discourses.

However, there was evidence of change that contributed to a general challenge to the current social order. Radical changes occurred at the local level and within the site of subjectivity through shifting positions. Critical thinking created spaces for subjects to engage with radical discourses and theoretical positions.

> PB: *Have your attitudes and perspectives changed?*
>
> Hilda: *Definitely! I have learned to be more tolerant, patient, kinder. I was quite impatient before. I've learned people have different levels, backgrounds, and ideas but that doesn't mean they're not valid.*

Hilda is self-defined middle class and describes a life of privilege through her social class positioning. She was 'impatient' with (working-class) others; expecting everyone to approach situations the way she did. As a student such notions of class superiority were fundamentally challenged as she learned from the (mostly working-class) students in her classroom. She repeatedly observed that one of the main benefits of access education was meeting people from different backgrounds, raising her awareness that everyone's knowledge is different but equally valid.

The following extract is from a piece of work completed by Greg on the Return to Study course. It provides an example of one student's engagement with radical discourses as a tool for challenging dominant notions of success and failure:

> *During my time on the RTS course, I have been able to really allow myself to reflect on my life experiences.*
>
> *When I left school and went to work, mainly on building sites, I think I chose this area to work in because I felt the only skill I had was*

that I was 'good with my hands'. After two years I became self-employed through the influence of my father-in-law who owned his own business. Soon I was working for him as a supervisor and later as a Contracts Manager. My strengths of fairness, openness and honesty were severely challenged by the culture of the people I worked with. I found it extremely difficult to work within this system. Eventually I realised that I was going to have to conform to this culture if I was going to progress. For years I lived as I thought people expected me to live. To some extent it worked, but it was not really me. I did gain lots of new skills through having to negotiate my way through this system, as I thought at the time that this way of life did not come naturally to me. Over the years, as my wife had started a career in social work, our relationship developed as I started to become more confident in our shared beliefs. Eventually I was able to feel confident enough to start to be honest with myself. I started to make informed choices about myself. I am now able to be assertive in more situations as my self-confidence grows. It is a revelation when you start to realise your strengths as a person can also be your skills in your life, either in your working environment or social environment.

The reflexivity encouraged on Return to Study enabled Greg to reconsider his subjectivity and relationships. He reclaims the values or 'strengths' (fairness, openness and honesty) that had been previously undermined by the competitive culture of the building sites. He describes himself as trying in the name of 'progress' to fit in to a system he does not understand. This resonates with Hall's point that 'identity arises, not so much from the fullness of identity which is already inside us as individuals, but from a *lack* of wholeness which is 'filled' from *outside* us, by the ways we imagine ourselves to be seen by *others*' (Hall, 1992: 287-8, original emphases).

Greg's narrative vividly captures this process as he remembers trying so desperately 'to live as [he] thought people expected [him] to live'. It is through the informal learning process experienced with his wife, as she trained to be a social worker, that the radical discourses became available to him, and this was intensified by his participation on the Return to Study course. Greg often saw me before or after class to discuss the uncertainty and excitement with which he experienced these shifts in his subjectivity and understandings of the social world.

Conclusion

This chapter considered the participants' desire for self-discovery through education. The concept of subjectivity highlighted the fact that identity formation is a complex process. It revealed that the participants were multiply positioned and this was complicated by their participation in access courses. The negotiation of shifting and contradictory subjectivities generated dilemmas and confusions for them. Although the students experienced access education as empowering, it also caused pain and uncertainty at times.

Access education is not simply about progress and success. Progress itself has multiple and contested meanings, and the drive for success often creates anxiety. After all, the notion of success depends on the notion of failure. The popular expression 'you can't have winners without having losers' illustrates this dichotomy. So education is not a simple story 'with a happy ending' and it holds moments of pain and danger as well as moments of pleasure and reward. It creates possibilities for liberatory subject positions while simultaneously reproducing inequalities and exclusions.

We also saw that the participants often rejected the dominant discourses of education and had their own notions about what education meant to them. The chapter ended with a consideration of the participants taking up radical subject positions and discourses that challenge social injustices, a theme that will be explored further in the next chapter.

Notes

1 The palimpsest is a metaphor 'derived from the image of wiring on parchment, writing which is only partially erased to make way for new writing each previous writing, therefore, bumping into and shaping the reading of the next layer of writing. This metaphor is used to explain the ways in which the subject is written and overwritten through multiple and contradictory discourses' (Davies, 1997: 275).

2 I use 'radical' to mean 'those discourses/practices [and subject positions] seeking to challenge the legitimacy of the dominant order and break its hold over social life' (Lather, 1991: xv).

7
Resisting Radical Discourses

Masculinist epistemology and ways of doing business – whether in global politics, academic or office politics – is competitive, oppositional, and at its most rudimentary, it is war. As with most other disciplinary discourses, one is either 'in' or 'out' of the dominant camp. Feminist critiques of master discourses are by historical definition 'out'. In this divide and rule relation, academic debate is deferred as other (critical) voices are quickly positioned as opposing, contesting, and destructive forces which need to be silenced and put in their place by a verbal dressing down in the textual space of the rational counter-argument: the endless rejoinder. (Luke and Gore, 1992: 205)

Background and introduction
The rampant individualism of our culture is a barrier to social change and justice. It has become increasingly unfashionable to speak about 'social change', and 'social revolution'. Furthermore, the steady flow of distorting media images has created in the popular imagination a frightening image of 'feminists' and 'radicals' that discourages radical discourses.

On a recent Access to Humanities exam board, colleagues expressed their anxieties that the course would be closed in favour of the vocational Access courses which successfully recruited large numbers. Students reported that the Course had been empowering, trans-

117

formatory, hugely confidence-boosting and had raised their political consciousness. These are some of their students' comments:

> I didn't realise before that education is about being critical.
>
> The course teaches you to be critical, to think and analyse...things you need in the real world.
>
> All of us are doing this for the pleasure of learning, not for work reasons.
>
> The course made us look at things in a completely different way.
>
> Our relationship with tutors is dynamic and they really listen to what we have to say.
>
> (From Access to Humanities moderation reports 1997-2000)

Non-vocational access education is struggling to survive in the current political climate. A recent survey indicates that student numbers are declining on non-vocational Access courses (Field, 1999). This chapter considers how radical discourses are resisted within access education. This is explored in relation to my experiences as a feminist tutor and the participants' experiments with feminist subject positions at Ford College. The concept of 'micro-politics' (Ball, 1987) is used as an analytical tool to uncover the struggle in attempting to develop radical praxis.

The concept of micro-politics

This chapter focuses on micro-politics, to bring to light 'hidden meanings' and 'gendered processes of power' (Morley, 1999: 5). Blase (1991: 1) defines micro-politics as being...

> about power and how people use it to influence others and to protect themselves. It is about conflict and how people compete with each other to get what they want. It is about co-operation and how people build support among themselves to achieve their ends. (cited in Morley, 1999: 5)

What are the discourses in play within the College? How do some gain hegemony while others do not? An analysis of my research diary revealed the subtle ways my peers undermined radical practices and developments. It was through research reflexivity rather than the day-to-day practice as a feminist tutor that patterns emerged in terms of obstacles to developing radical pedagogy. When 200 leaflets for the Women's Studies course went missing, I did not at first connect it to the micro-politics of the department. Morley significantly points out that:

> Like many aspects of racial and gender oppression, bullying and sexual harassment at work, micro-politics can also be subtle, elusive, volatile, difficult to capture, leaving individuals unsure of the validity of their readings of a situation. What appears trivial in a single instance requires new significance when located within a wider analysis of power relations. The attribution of meaning and decoding of transactions, locations and language is an important component of micro-politics. Both feminism and micro-politics privilege processes rather than structures. Both can label unnamed feelings, experiences, practices and transactions, because the language in which oppressed groups express these phenomena is often politically and socially subjugated and rendered irrelevant or illegitimate by dominant discourses. (*ibid.*: 5-6)

Feminists 'need both to read organisational micro-politics and evolve their own micropolitical strategies for intervention and change'. An exploration of micro-politics 'exposes subterranean conflicts and the minutiae of social relations' (*ibid.*):

> The exercising of power in organisations can be overt and identifiable, but also subtle, complex and confusing. Blase and Anderson (1995: 13) suggest that in a postmodern world, power is used and structured into social relations so that it does not appear to be 'used at all. The cultural and feminist approach to micro-politics of organisational life contributes to an understanding of the distorting effects of power and the ways that power is exercised invisibly' (Marshall and Anderson, 1994: 175). A micropolitical analysis renders the competition and domination visible; exposing processes of stalling, sabotage, manipulation, power bargaining, bullying, harassment and spite. (*ibid.*)

The chapter examines attempts to develop radical and collaborative approaches to access education at Ford College, focusing on the micro-politics of the College and the struggles between dominant and radical discourses.

Active other/ing

My research diary reveals a pattern that highlights how feminist tutors might be actively othered and positioned outside of 'legitimate' discourses. Our attempts to practise empowering pedagogies, to subvert conventional power relations and to develop collaborative methodologies were actively othered, so reinforcing stereotypes of radical discourses as dangerous and perverse. The following extract describes a team meeting held just after I had been written up in a local paper for winning a national award. The article disclosed my experiences of surviving a violent marriage. This public disclosure shaped the exchanges in our team meeting:

Today we had a team meeting about developing the Return to Study year two course. Jan Reed immediately had patronising words to say to me. 'I saw your five minutes of fame in the paper' she told me. Celia Lance was listening carefully – she had not seen the article herself. Jan asked me how I felt about the personal bits and I told her I had made a decision to speak publicly about the issue as I was determined not to collude in hiding domestic violence as though it were a private matter. She replied that she felt it had been 'inappropriate' and that I was not presenting an image as a 'manager in charge of over 100 students'. I appeared 'weak', she argued, and 'vulnerable' and 'personal problems should be dealt with through inner strength and not talked about again and again'.

I explained that my reasons for speaking out were political: that domestic violence was not a personal problem nor a private issue, and as long as it was regarded as such, thousands of women would remain in danger. I said it took courage and strength to speak about it publicly and added that I would never wish to subscribe to the model of management she was referring to and that I wanted to be perceived not as an authority figure but as a woman who had experiences that other women could relate to, an approachable person. I wanted to create some sense of equality in my relationships with staff and students. After all, I added, the programme was for groups who had experienced material disadvantages, may have low levels of self-confidence and who might themselves have experienced domestic violence. She remarked that I had the mis-

conception that Return to Study students were victims. Before Jan or I could say more, Cynthia Webb joined us, and we began the agenda of the team meeting. (Research Diary 3 February 1998)

Valerie Hey uses the concept of the 'hidden curriculum vitae' (Cohen, 1999) to represent 'a resistant act towards those who would erase the difference of 'past lives'' (Hey, 2000: 172). Jan, positioning herself within the discourse of professionalism, tried to erase my 'past life' on the basis that reference to it was inappropriate to my position as manager. The discourse between us felt combative (Maher and Tetreault, 1994), because my colleague aligned herself firmly with masculinist models of management and authority, against my 'weak' and 'vulnerable' public 'confessions'. The fact that male violence touches a significant number of women's lives was denied, although teaching mature women students has shown me otherwise. Her insistence that domestic violence was simply a personal problem warned me that I was stepping outside of main-stream discourses of what it means to be a FE manager. The ex-change had to be negotiated in the public language of the profes-sional meeting, a language that served to privilege Jan's disapproval of attempts to speak about the 'unspeakable' in public forums (Ribbens and Edwards, 1998; Mauthner, 1998b: 45).

Jan's discourse individualised the gendered experiences of women and rendered them invisible. Her denial of the structural constraints and disadvantages experienced by many Return to Study students, re-privileged the ideology of individualism and meritocracy, and the patriarchal separation of the private and public spheres of life. Feminists have revealed how the separation of the private and public perpetuate women's inequality and powerlessness, by excluding their experiences and needs from the public/political arena of social life (Ribbens and Edwards, 1998). Patriarchal ways of being, think-ing and speaking are upheld, while feminist ones are positioned as abnormal, deviant and unprofessional.

Jan's claim that I appeared weak and vulnerable in the eyes of 'insiders', raises the question of why many women feel safer align-ing themselves with a masculinist position, while 'actively othering' women who do not. Foucault named such processes 'technologies of normalisation': attempts to regulate any deviations from established social· norms (Rabinow, 1984: 20-22). As Alison Jones explains, individuals are...

> less likely to take up alternative rather than prevailing subject positions. This is because the dominant positions are embedded in the sets of meanings which define what is 'ordinary' and what we might take for granted about, say, gender. The 'alternative' or oppositional positions are not seen by girls [or women] as desirable – or even possible – alternatives. (Jones, 1993: 161)

Silencing radical pedagogies

Dominant discourses also positioned students as 'the outsider'. Dorothy often felt silenced and 'othered' as a student and mother and these feelings were intensified while she was taking a teacher training course. She had first returned to education three years earlier, after many years of battling with the school system for support for her dyslexic son. As a concerned mother, she joined the Dyslexic Association but could not participate in meetings because of the jargon used, which excluded those outside the professional boundaries. She became determined to learn more about dyslexia so she could further her son's case and came to the College.

> *I went to a meeting, there were a few head teachers, a few educational psychologists...it was quite a big meeting and I sat there and I felt like although I'm here I'm not here. I felt like I'm over there looking in. Because they were all talking in this terminology that I didn't understand. And the day I walked out of that meeting I thought I've got to find all this out for his sake more that anything. I went to the Dyslexic Association and said I want to learn more. How can I go about learning more? And they said well there's courses at Y College. You had to be interviewed and everything and it was a big palaver and at the time my Dad wasn't well. I went to the interview but I couldn't go on the course. I put it off for a year. Then I found out that this College was doing the course. It was basically a Learning Support programme based on Dyslexia. (Dorothy, 1999)*

After completing the course, Dorothy continued at the College, studying Word Power, Return to Study, GCSE Humanities and

English. After a few months of working voluntarily in the College as a classroom assistant, she was employed as a support worker. This led her to take the teacher training course, where she felt her advocacy of dyslexic students was being undermined. To illustrate this, she described her experience of presenting a micro-session, an assessed teaching exercise of 20 minutes.

Dorothy: *[The tutor] says all these, you know, vary your teaching methods, give praise where it's due and he never does. We've been in there since September and only now are we just starting to get to know each other. I could so easily have got into a political row with him the other day.*

PB: *Tell me about that.*

Dorothy: *I did the micro-session on dyslexia. At first I explained about the brain and dyslexia. Then I went on to umm, I had the overhead projector and then, first I went through the facts provided by the Dyslexic Association...umm, and then I pulled three people up for a role play. It was completely varied, I did the overhead projector, the hand-outs, equipment used to help dyslexic students... anyway I pulled three people up and the first one I asked to read a hand-out written in Chinese aloud to the class. And I acted like a strict teacher asking 'Why can't you read it? You have to read it!' and the tutor only thought I was being rude! And umm, before I finished I said that 'as teachers of adults you should be aware that some of these people have had a lot of difficulties at school and they do bear scars from school'. So when I finished, it was the feedback session and the tutor said I was giving conflicting information. And then he said, he sort of said I should get my facts straight, he said 'one minute you're saying it's genes and then you're saying it's to do with the way people have been treated at school' and...*

PB: *But the feedback session isn't supposed to be about the content of your session, it's supposed to be about your teaching strategies, so why was he drilling you about your subject?*

Dorothy: *Because it's dyslexia again. I don't know what it is...I get the feeling that they think I'm some sort of witch doctor spreading all these terrible rumours that the education system doesn't cater for underachieving kids.*

PB: *Which is the truth, that's what happens...and actually what your saying is that it's not the dyslexic students who are the problem...*

Dorothy: *It is the truth. So what I quoted to him – I said at the moment 45% of prisoners are dyslexic and he gave me such a look! And the Dyslexic Association is trying to help these prisoners to read and write. And if he'd allowed me to go on...I did say to him, it's all to do with league tables as well. I said these schools have to show these league tables that they're performing well, and to have all these disruptive underachieving kids is no good for them so they find all ways to get them out. So what happens – they end up on the streets and eventually in prison. Anyway, he went on and then he hands out three bits of paper to get feedback from the class. And the feedback from the class was just unreal. They all thought it was very good. And then the following week another student did his micro session on knots! Everyone laughed because when we got hand-outs with all these bits of string and all that to try to do these knots...see now if he had started the session off with why he was interested in this, we would have had a better understanding. If he started out explaining he climbs mountains so it's life saving...*

PB: *How did you find that out then?*

Dorothy: *Because the tutor did say at the end that if he started off telling us... but that's what I mean – you're never right, because when I spoke about dyslexia I started off with why I was interested in it and a couple of times I referred to my son – and he said at the end 'how do you feel about her using her family as an example?' The class thought it was good, but I got the sense that he felt I shouldn't use my family. He made me feel I should never ever use my family as an example and yet the next week he's telling this bloke that he should start off with why he's interested...*

PB: *You should've stood up and said 'aren't you a bit contradictory?'* [laugh]

Dorothy: *I feel I really should stand up and say loads of things but I've got to the point now where I think 'oh just keep your mouth shut, it's not worth it'. Because he'll come back with something else.* (Dorothy, 1999)

Dorothy is undermined when she draws on her experiences of mothering a dyslexic son. The other student is advised to bring attention to his personal interest. Yet Dorothy's personal interest is constructed as illegitimate because it is located in the feminised realm of the private, and that is forbidden to appear in public fields such as the classroom. The tutor seizes the opportunity to juxtapose acceptable (masculine) interests against unacceptable (feminine) interests in the context of 'appropriate' teaching behaviour. He appears to go to lengths to weaken her attempts to raise critical awareness amongst student teachers from a perspective of dyslexic students. Dorothy is positioned as the confused subject who has her 'facts' wrong and who illegitimately draws on personal experience.

Dorothy and I shared a commonality of experience. Both of us struggled to raise critical awareness and develop pedagogical approaches that challenged dominant regimes of truth.

On the outside looking in

There was a strong professional ethic within the access programmes at Ford College that demanded a distanced, objective and neutral position. Yet my experiences as a mature student, as a mother, as a survivor of domestic violence, were useful stories to share in the project of widening participation. Drawing attention to power relations helps reveal the micro-politics of access education. Radical approaches to curriculum development and pedagogy disrupt the practices that reinforce privilege and exclusions. Emphasising the subjective and personal in the production of knowledge integrates a politics of difference into classroom dynamics and enables students to contribute to reconstructing theory and meaning. Collaborative research provided a space for participants to refashion methodology, pedagogy and epistemology.

Conventional relations of power between teacher and student were destabilised through radical discourses. This provoked disapproval because the certainties of the teacher-authority which many depend upon in the classroom were explicitly challenged. The following 'memory work' illustrates these issues:

*By the time of launching the Women's Studies course, I was dis-
advantaged by my marginal status in the College as a part-time
lecturer. My colleagues had opposed the course from its very be-
ginnings. I proposed that the course should provide a woman-only
space, offered as a three-hour per week option on the Access to
Higher Education and Return to Study programmes. My colleagues
protested on the grounds that I was excluding male students. I
argued that male students could participate on any of the many
other courses provided, and we could always develop a special
male-only class if it were required. However, I argued that it was
necessary for women students, after years of having their achievements and experiences marginalised, to have a space provided for
them to feel safe about exploring their pasts and making sense of
their experiences through the body of feminist theory available to
them. Ironically, both male senior managers supported the course,
while my female peers were opposed to the idea[1]. Perhaps due to
such strong managerial support, the team finally agreed that we
would provide Women's Studies as a course for women.*

*Later on in the year, I was accused, this time by a male peer, of
breaching the equal opportunities policy by excluding men. As a
part-time member of staff, I was not invited to participate in team
meetings, so heard these accusations only at second-hand. I could
not understand how it could be acceptable for me to be excluded
from meetings about the course I was responsible for organising,
while simultaneously being accused of causing exclusion. My
feminist position placed me outside of the professional discourse,
stereotyped as (a reverse) sexist, yet denied a public voice to
represent the course I developed, taught and organised. At no time
was I invited to discuss the Women's Studies course on an equal
footing with my peers; I was systematically excluded from any
opportunities to explain my pedagogical approaches and philo-
sophies. Through e-mails – by this time my only way of com-
municating with my line manager – I argued for the need to protect
this woman-only space and to develop a separate space for men to
explore issues of gender in relation to their experiences as men.
The message I received in response was supportive but the strong
support I had initially received as a full-time member of staff had
clearly weakened.*

> *'Your ideas for men's studies very much fit into my thinking, though I'm not having a lot of response from the team on that one (or even women's studies for that matter...). I shall see what I can do!'*

> *I knew the only chance I had to ensure Women's Studies would survive was by recruiting an impressive number of students. But as a part-time tutor, I did not have access to incoming students. I requested permission to attend an approaching Open Evening in order to present the course. My students offered to attend with me, to share their experiences of the course with potential students. We made a beautiful poster together and wrote a piece collectively to reflect the strengths of the course. I was sent a message that it was inappropriate for me, as a part-time member of staff, to attend the Open Evening, and I should simply supply my colleagues with the appropriate publicity material. Following the Open Evening, I was told there had been no enquiries for Women's Studies.*

The micro-politics inherent in the above[2] reveal the struggles that serve as a barrier to the development of radical approaches to teaching and learning. The appropriation of radical concepts, in this case 'sexism', serves as a weapon against feminist agendas in the patriarchal battle to maintain the status quo. As women's presence has increased within educational institutions, denial grows that feminism is still needed (Walter, 1998: 2). It has become part of popular understanding that British women have not only achieved social equality, but are now doing better than men (*ibid.*: 1-9). Indeed, at widening participation conferences and College staff meetings, there have been numerous pleas for access advocates to turn their attention away from women and re-focus their energies on men.

Access education has successfully recruited a large number of women, transforming the gender profile in higher education. However, evidence shows that women continue to experience material and social inequalities. Within further education, women are concentrated in traditionally feminine areas, including beauty, administrative, social science and community care courses, preparing women for their entry into low-paid 'feminised' work (Uden, 1996). Women academics are concentrated in lower status positions and make up the majority of part-time staff (Gardiner and O'Rourke, 1998:133). On average, female academics earn £4000 less per year than male academics (EOC, 2000). On average in the UK, the gap between the hourly pay of men and women working full time is 18% (ibid.) and women working part time earn about half the average hourly pay of men working full time (Grimshaw and Rubery, 2001).

Such evidence supports women-only provision (Coats, 1994; Elsdon *et al*, 1995). Elsdon *et al* argue the value of women-only provision, drawing on their study of learning within voluntary organisations:

> Belonging to something which is especially for them has a particular value... Most [interviewees] felt that they are able to be 'more frank' in the absence of men. In women's groups 'women can be in charge', 'they blossom, aren't edged out by men. Women on their own were considered 'more supportive' of each other, 'interested and caring', and observers as well as members noted the freedom from competition in their groups. There was also a distinct absence of any sense of ritualistic structure or behaviour, and of hierarchy, in all-woman groups.

> Important as they were in general, these characteristics of women-only groups were seen to be most significant at periods of major role change. Some examples of...social learning supported by the group at these times drew on the period of isolation experienced by so many women when they have young families. Group support was enabling them to cope, to maintain a sense of identity, proportion and of wider horizons. At the stage of emergence from exclusive domesticity, and suffering from almost universal loss of confidence in facing the 'outside' world and its tasks, women's groups were reported to be of special value, as they were again when supporting individuals preparing for a new or resumed career and making the requisite changes. (Elsdon *et al,* 1995: 56-57 quoted in McGivney, 1998: 13)

From my personal exchanges with other feminist tutors, it appears the ideological weapons used to undermine the development of radical discourses, pedagogies and approaches are widespread. Women often hesitate to take courses associated with feminism because they feel, with good reason, they will be risking their chances of 'success' rather than enhancing them. Many women, due to the material inequalities that continue to exist and deepen, come to education because they are in highly vulnerable situations. They may be at risk of losing benefits and have little time to invest in education before finding paid work. However, they are at risk of finding employment in the informal sector, characterised by the 'house-wifization of labour' (Hart, 1992; see Chapter Two). Without the radical education to help make sense of their gendered experiences, women may not discover the root causes but see their hardships as self-inflicted; their fault, their 'failures'.

Denial as a survival strategy

Confronting oppression and inequality is a painful journey of critical awareness in relation to self, subjectivity and social world.

> Lynsey: *I must admit that I'm really pleased that I did stay with this Women's Studies course, because I was really in a terrible state through the feminist...*
>
> PB: *theory?*
>
> Lynsey: *Yeah, yeah, I couldn't handle it and I was gonna walk out.*
>
> Shelley: *Really?*
>
> PB: *So, why, why was it so difficult? Explain, explain what it was...*
>
> Lynsey: *I don't know, I think the issues that we were dealing with, and the low self-esteem and the lack of confidence –*
>
> Shelley: *Did you feel that we were being hostile to men? Being that you've got such a secure –*
>
> Lynsey: *No, no no! No, I think it was bringing up issues – right, even though I'd faced the issues, of my childhood and everything else, it was still, I think it was the actual talking about it with other women...* (Women's Studies group discussion, 1999)

Women's Studies starts from women's perspectives and experiences.[3] These are often painful, as well as empowering, places to start. Women's experiences and relations are 'socially invisible' (Mauthner, 1998b: 39), locked into the silent space of the personal and private. Speaking about such socially taboo issues as abuse, the contradictions of mothering, depression, low self-esteem, sexuality and desire, often causes guilt, pain and fear and is enmeshed in risk and danger. Such 'socially invisible' experiences are contradictory, confusing, multiple and fluid. Confronting painful experiences of oppression takes courage. Doing so often leaves women feeling vulnerable after the mechanisms of denial that have been built up over years of learning how to survive in a misogynist, patriarchal and capitalist society are shattered.

> Shelly: *Umm, one thing I think that's quite sad about the group, is that they're all, all of us are people coming from the same wave-length. And people that haven't really been on that wave-length have been lost.*
>
> PB: *Mm*
>
> Shelly: *I find that sad, in – in the – the whole thing as a subject, that needs looking into. Is it always going to attract people who've got that vision? Because I'd like to think that, umm, obviously education...*
>
> Kate: *What vision?*
>
> Shelly: *You know that sight into life, that openness...*
>
> Kate: *Looking for more...*
>
> Shelly: *You know, they can see things more, they're not all tunnelled. You know there's a lot of people that would go around and they're just quite happy to be blinkered and not to look for ways, for whatever reasons, it might be fear, insecurity, umm, quite 'I'm ok chap, happy' whatever, and I'm getting good marks, where some people like – that isn't enough for them and also they're gonna ask why and question and that perhaps we all are that way and we want to challenge things and change things. I'm not saying we're all the same, because we're not all the same, but I'd say there is something in there, that light...*
>
> PB: *There is a sharing of a goal?*
>
> Shelly: *Yeah, there is something there – there, like you say Penny, that we all share, that has brought us there. What saddens me is that the people that aren't there are the people that have dropped*

out of – I remember one particular lady whose dropped out very early on, who had a lot of trouble with ideas and things.

PB: *Yes*

Shelly: *But the – the class didn't capture people like that.*

PB: *Why do you think it didn't capture her? Why do you think she left? If we think about that individual student...*

Shelly: *I think she probably couldn't hack the umm, the – where we were coming from. I feel that she saw it as hostile, or threatening to her own life and how she was with her husband and with her family and things.*

Kate: *Happy with what she knew – didn't want it disrupted.*

(Women's Studies group discussion, 1999)

Denial operates as a protective shield. Although a feminist goal is women's empowerment, identification with feminism and other radical discourses necessitates a position on the margins and so involves relinquishing the safety of 'insider positions'. As Skeggs argues in relation to the white, working-class women she studied,

> a movement into middle-class White feminism may involve the complete loss of all that has been invested in, a loss of the only cultural capital they have and know, a movement into a place where they are unlikely to have respect. (1997: 155)

The journey a woman experiences on a Women's Studies course requires shifts in thinking from dominant to radical discourses. Such shifts are dramatic and traumatic, and often involve significant and frightening challenges to lifestyles, identities and relationships.

> *I'm not a feminist really, in a way, I mean I don't believe that men should run women down, and abuse them completely. I think they should, there should be a balance. But then I'm a little bit old fashioned as well. You know, like I think a woman should do the house purely because she's better at it, I suppose really, and a man should go out and earn the money. But then I've got like the old fashioned values that I think fit quite nicely with modern ones and they aren't too extreme. (Vanessa, 1999)*

Vanessa's comments are made while she is struggling to maintain her marriage after a brief separation. The separation was provoked by the identifications and subject positions newly available to her through education that caused frictions with the discursive position of 'wife'. Feminist ideas were clearly antagonistic to her battle to maintain her marriage and so she continued to produce herself through heterosexual discourses that naturalise the domestic division of labour. Vanessa chose to reject feminism for more liberal middle-of-the-road discourses that resolved the conflict between radical positions and conservative ones. This way she could position herself as 'a modern woman' while maintaining her identification with conventional versions of housewife and mother, thus negotiating the balance required for her to survive the world of home as well as the world of College.

Conclusion

In exploring the micro-politics at Ford College, this chapter demonstrated how radical discourses are resisted. Concepts such as active othering reveal the struggles between insider and outsider discourses, and the ways in which peers replace those identifying with feminism firmly on the outside. The mainstream separation of the private and public spheres operates to silence and render invisible women's experiences and perspectives of the world. Those who seek to make public women's experiences must do so in the absence of a language to express the personal. Women students who engage with feminist ideas do so at the risk of being 'othered' and of breaking down the shields of denial that have served to protect them from confronting the realities of oppression. Exploring women's experiences and identifying with feminist and radical discourses is a journey of mixed pain and pleasure, yet paved with emancipatory possibilities.

Notes

1   The embodiment of gender does not necessarily translate into the adoption of feminist or anti-feminist positions and discourses. Many men draw on feminist theory to make sense of their working, personal, intellectual and emotional subjectivities, while many women position themselves firmly as anti-feminist.

2   This is my version of events from my perspective at the time of writing it. Written accounts of memories are selective and partial and do not reveal 'the truth'. Memories are always constructions of how we understand our selves and our situations at a precise moment of time and are shaped by historical, political and social contexts. Such understanding is constantly shifting through dynamic discourses.

3   Although I do not believe there is one universal 'women's experience', I would argue that the patriarchal separation of the private and the public conceals the similarities between different groups of women. Male violence is one example of an experience shared by many women, although there are differences between women's experience of male violence in relation to age, class, dis/ability, nationality and race.

8

Conclusions:
Accessing Possibilities

In life, I feel too much emphasis is put on qualifications and not enough thought put into identifying people's personal skills. The Return to Study programme, together with my life experiences, has enabled me to identify an area in which I would like to work. This work would entail raising a person's self-esteem and enabling others to value the diversity of individuals. (Greg, coursework, Return to Study, 1998)

Collaborative approaches within Access Education

To widen participation effectively, Access education has to be collaboratively refashioned. It needs to be imbued with interactive approaches to methodology and pedagogy that give students a sense of ownership and control over research and learning processes.

The teacher-as-researcher approach adds rich dimensions, and complexities, to research and pedagogical relations. It opens possibilities for developing collaboration with students in all aspects of the research and learning process. Collaboration enables co-participants to reflexively discuss, critique and develop empowering and inclusive approaches to teaching and learning. Methodology and pedagogy become closely connected.

A reflexive approach to widening participation addresses difference and context and contributes to anti-discriminatory educational practices. Research is used as a pedagogical tool for developing approaches in which access students are included in the negotiation of their classroom cultures and learning experiences. The classroom provides a space for students to critique pedagogy, and this produces data and facilitates collaborative analysis. Processes and relations are the dominant issues for consideration so there is less emphasis on methods. This encourages students to actively reshape their learning experiences in collaboration with their teacher. 'Providing a more accurate and valid representation of local people's experiences' (Dockery, 2000: 97) enhances the quality of the research.

Deconstructing discourses of access education

This book has traced some of the contradictions and conflicts in the practices, relations and discourses of widening participation. Competing discourses were shown to create tensions between access teachers at Ford College because of the different versions of 'being an access teacher' which were actively constructed. The meaning of access education was contested and refashioned, producing a range of contradictory positions for the access students and staff. By tracing competing discourses, the book has identified the contradictory positions available to access students and teachers that generate dilemmas for their sense of self and has revealed the nuances and complexities of the lived world of access education, a world marked by confusions and contradictions and uneasy partnerships between radical politics and academic traditions.

The competing meanings of educational access

Today I bumped into Linda at the school. She explained that her teachers were frequently asking her about her future plans regarding work. One of her teachers suggested that with her computing courses she could go into secretarial work. Linda said she wasn't sure what she wanted to do – except to keep studying. She felt she didn't know what she would do if she had to stop studying now. She explained that learning for her was something so much deeper than work skills. (Research Diary, May 2000)

Dominant notions of widening participation have overshadowed the radical project of access education for social justice. Lifelong learning is identified as a key solution to national economic regeneration and welfare reformation. Individual citizens are expected to take up opportunities to learn new skills to prepare for and take up employment. Values of individual enterprise, risk-taking and competitiveness are privileged through the hegemonic discourse of widening participation. Locating problems such as poverty and social exclusion within the (dependent) individual, the discourse ignores the fact that British history is rooted in colonialism and institutional classism, racism and sexism. This discourse upholds the notion of a meritocratic society in which enterprising individuals grab opportunities presumed to be equally available to all, to improve their futures by progressing through education and into work. It operates to render invisible the ways that it repositions subjects as classed, raced and gendered, thereby facilitating the reproduction of social inequalities and exclusions.

The discourse of widening participation may therefore even exacerbate social exclusions. Hart's (1992) adaptation of the 'housewifization of labour' shows that many access students are in danger of being steered into the contemporary conditions of marginal waged labour (see Chapter Two). Through Government initiatives to widen educational participation, 'the unemployed' will be forced to take up instrumentally oriented courses, which focus on Basic and Key Skills, to get them off welfare benefits and into work that is often low paid, part-time and casual. New Labour claims that a 'risk society' is a good solution to social exclusion (Giddens, 1998). The underlying assumption is that risk-taking pays off, individually and nationally, (Hodgson, 2000: 52-53) while the social security system leads to unhealthy levels of dependence. We need further research that develops an understanding of the risk-assessment calculations made by students when they are making decisions about participating in education or not.

The government has replaced student grants with loans, while contradictorily portraying widening participation as a key strategy for future national stability. In their attempt to benefit from educational opportunities, access students will continue to be forced by such policy into increasingly stressful situations that might be dangerous to their health. Further research is needed to examine the implications of the new funding policy for mature students' chances to access further and higher education. True commitment to widening participation would require policy makers to take full account of the effects of adult learning on the personal finances, relations, subjectivities and family dynamics of mature students.

The discursive construction of access students as 'non-standard' and inferior

Although access education seeks to empower marginalised groups, its location in the academic world often repositions access students as inferior and exacerbates their feelings of anxiety. Such feelings are generated by the educational practices and discourses in the academic world that re-inscribe and re-construct subjects across and within systems of inequality based on age, class, ethnicity, gender and physical ability.

The participants' accounts regularly revealed that educational experiences were characterised by intimidation and fear. Returning to a formal institution of education produced feelings of anxiety, rooted in the mechanisms of exclusion that serve to position certain groups as not worthy of serious academic pursuit (see Chapter Five). Discourses of selectivity categorise access students as 'non-standard' and illegitimate, and students from marginalised groups are defined in terms of these discourses (Williams, 1997a). At all stages of the access education process these students are constructed and re-constructed as inferior to the 'norm' – the 18-year-old 'A' level student. Discourses of selectivity reinforce these constructions and they are repeatedly re-emphasised through discourses of standards and standardisation and struggles over rights to access. These discourses produce access students as 'equal but different', yet their difference is consistently measured against the 'normal' and 'standard' student.

The book also draws attention to the intimidating practices of access education, most particularly in relation to pedagogy. These are important: they affect students' learning and lives. The discourse of standards and standardisation is upheld by certain pedagogical approaches such as examinations. Exams often serve to re-privilege particular groups as 'knowers' and maintain unequal power relationships within a naturalised hierarchy that depends for its maintenance on particular regimes of truth. Examinations are assumed to be the obvious solution to the problem of standards and standardisation. But the processes by which examinations serve as a device of 'disciplinary power' are ignored and hidden (Foucault, 1975, 1984) and instead they are constructed as the objective measurement of achievement (Canaan, 1997). The notion of 'achievement' itself is not critiqued but is understood as a universal ideal that is free from values, politics and cultural associations. Thus is the popular assumption that Britain is a meritocratic society re-inforced and the reality that inequalities and exclusions are discursively, structurally and systematically reproduced within institutions such as colleges and universities concealed.

I am not arguing that examinations should never be used in access education or that access education is an intimidating process that reinforces every student's feelings of inferiority. It is important that access students are included in the same educational practices as other students (and vice versa). However, the idea that examinations are always a good thing for *any* student because they are objective and fair measurements of achievement must be critically interrogated. I am arguing for a reflexive approach to widening participation that places access students and their experiences at the centre of the project to develop more effective and inclusive strategies in future. In order to widen participation, particular cultural practices that are rooted in regimes of truth serving the most powerful must be critiqued and challenged. My research diary account of a recent conversation with a participant illustrates my point:

Today I walked home from the school with Linda. We chatted about her Return to Study course. She is now in her third year at the College, doing the third component of the programme developed by the new Return to Study Programme Manager. It is an AS level, rather than an Open College Network course. It is multi-disciplinary, although not interdisciplinary, as it does not focus on the connections between subjects. Linda is worried about the examinations she has to sit to pass this course in June. Her fear of exams, she explained, may cause her to draw a blank. I asked her whether she was nevertheless enjoying the course. She replied that in a way she was but she wished they would spend more time concentrating on one subject, with greater depth rather than breadth. She felt too much emphasis rested on completing assignments quickly in order to gain the qualification, rather than on the learning process that motivated her to continue at College. She complained that they were touching on too many different subjects and consequently not getting much out of anything. Her other frustration was directly related to pedagogy. She could not get to grips with learning by taking notes off the board while the teacher talked. Although she spoke to the teacher about this, nothing had changed. However, she was adamant that she did not expect the teacher to change her teaching style just for her sake. (Research Diary, 15 March 2001)

Shifting subjectivities through educational participation

There is contradiction within the discourse of widening participation. Although it focuses on 'the excluded', it also constructs the British education system as based on equal opportunity and meritocracy, where all individuals may learn to become 'active citizens'. Access students are reproduced through positioned discourses of selectivity as classed, gendered and raced while simultaneously being reconstructed through the shifting discourses available through educational participation. In particular, students are now constructed as 'consumers of education', as equal players in the free market of adult education.

It is important to understand the implications of the multiple discourses that educational participation presents to students. Access students often return to study in a search for self-discovery. However, the changes created, exacerbated and left unresolved through learning generate painful dilemmas for them – as well as exciting possibilities. The educational project is too seldom experienced as progressive or empowering but is rather a source of conflicting emotions and meanings. Educational participation may generate contradictory subjectivities that cause fractures rather than closures, confusions rather than certainties. Learning may simultaneously be experienced as liberating and oppressive as access students encounter new ideas that challenge past securities, perceptions and identifications.

The participants in my study experienced a contradiction between the sense of a fixed and stable self and the sense of a shifting and multiple subjectivity. The dominant discourse of widening participation constructs access students as responsible citizens who have capitalised on their rights to learning, in order to improve themselves and their families. Structural inequalities such as class and gender are written out of this discourse, while lifelong learning opportunities are presented as available to all citizens who take the rational choice to gain credentials to improve their prospects within (waged) work. Unpaid work such as mothering is not recognised or validated as 'real work' and is only valued when supported by a breadwinner partner within a heterosexual relationship. Gender relations within the family are concealed. Educational participation is constructed as an instrumental action within the neo-liberal project of individual progress and success through market opportunities. Yet access students often reject these instrumental notions of education.

The book has explored the possibilities of mobilising radical discourses through access education. Data shows that the subject position of 'intelligent knower' had been made unavailable to access students throughout their lives because of the dominant discourses that reinforced structural and institutional inequalities. The collaborative approach enabled co-participants to explore the ways different subject positions were un-available to us in relation to age, class, dis/ability, ethnicity, gender, institutional status and race. The co-participants were able to play with radical discourses and practices, collectively deconstructing and critiquing them in light of our own experiences of education. Yet doing this through collaborative approaches, raised levels of resistance in the College to our classroom and research practices.

Micro-politics and the resistance of radical discourses

We have seen how co-participants made various attempts to mobilise radical discourses at Ford College, to challenge ways of knowing and thinking that reinforce social inequalities and exclude the experiences and ideas of access students. Why were feminist discourses actively resisted by my peers and, to a smaller extent, by students? The concept 'micro-politics' (Morley, 1999; Ball, 1987; Hoyle, 1982) was employed to reveal the subterranean struggles that occurred between staff who subscribed to different discursive positions. My peers adopted the conventional teacher-position, which depended on playing out a patriarchal discourse of professionalism, legitimate authority[1] and appropriate 'teacherly' behaviour. My position as a feminist was often undermined as the illegitimate position, and this at times sabotaged efforts to develop critical praxis for the project of widening participation. I struggled to create a feminist space for women students to explore their experiences and relationship to the world. Keeping a research diary enabled me to identify the subtle ways in which my development work at the College was continually undermined. Some of these might have otherwise been too subtle to take seriously or even to notice. A close analysis of micro-politics reveals the intricate ways that feminist subjects may be actively othered by those who attempt to regulate any deviations from established social norms through strategies of normalisation.

Access education needs to include access students in the production of knowledge and meaning making. Access education should provide opportunities for challenging the dominant discourses that reproduce social injustice. But how can this be possibile when hegemonic discourses have so much purchase for both access teachers and access students?

Access education is a site of struggle over meanings. This has been demonstrated by tracing the competing discourses that shape access provision, the different ways that access education is understood and valued and the shifting subjectivities of access students themselves. Examining the micro-politics of access education is important because it maps out these tacit struggles and makes them explicit.

Research about access education must reveal these hidden struggles in order to mobilise radical discourses that legitimise students' experiences and enable them to contribute actively to the production of meaning.

The micro-politics presented in this book are based on my versions of events. I did not collect my colleagues' perspectives in my study, and so they could not be presented here. However, my account illustrates the importance of examining micro-politics to help to explain the processes by which discourses become dominant or marginal, and how positions of risk or safety, power or vulnerability are discursively produced to create or prevent possibilities for change.

Effectively widening participation

Let us consider some practical strategies for effectively widening participation. The experiences and critiques of the co-participants in my study shape the following suggestions. Classroom dynamics are always produced by multiple and shifting social factors, and this necessitates that teachers and learners be reflexive and flexible in response to the specific contexts in which they are located. Thus there are no universal sets of practices that will automatically lead to effectively widening participation. There are, however, useful approaches that serve as a resource in developing inclusive educational practices that undermine exclusion and inequality. My suggestions fall into two categories: advice for access tutors and advice for access students, although these naturally overlap.

Access tutors

It is very important that a supportive and friendly learning environment is established early on in an access course. Students need to feel comfortable about exploring new and developing ideas in the classroom and this means that all classroom participants will sometimes makes mistakes or have difficulty in expressing themselves as they engage with unfamiliar concepts. Students often remember being humiliated in past educational contexts and it is crucial that they realise that making mistakes is a normal part of the learning process. Furthermore, it is important that tutors admit that they too are always learning and also make mistakes. Tutors should position themselves in the classroom as learners who are deconstructing and refashioning theories and knowledges collaboratively with their students.

A discussion of past experiences of learning helps to develop a supportive and reflexive learning environment early on in a course. Students consider their positive and negative educational experiences in small groups and construct a list of key aspects that make learning a positive experience. The whole class then reconvenes to share their ideas and negotiate a class agreement about pedagogical approaches. This should be reviewed, re-evaluated and renegotiated at regular intervals during the course.

Evaluation should be a continual reflexive tool in improving classroom practices and relations to combat exclusion – not just a questionnaire collected in the last fifteen minutes of the final lesson. Evaluation is initiated in the type of exercise that I describe directly above, which can be regularly addressed through various pedagogical approaches, such as using seminar journals for collaborative evaluation. The students and tutor keep individual journals of their reflections on classroom sessions. They write about their feelings and observations, considering teaching and learning strategies, classroom relationships, power relations, resources, support mechanisms and so on. The journals are regularly used in small group discussions as a resource to evaluate how the course is going. Critiques are then pooled together in a feedback session and tutor and students can collaboratively address any emerging problems or concerns. Strengths in classroom practices should also be highlighted and built upon.

Interactive pedagogical approaches are also crucial in effectively widening participation. Lectures are problematic because they reinforce the power relations between tutor and student and legitimate the tutor's knowledge as superior. In a lecture situation, the tutor is positioned as active and the students as passive. Whole class discussions are also a problem because the less confident students are more likely to keep silent, so unequal power relations are reproduced. This does not mean to say that the tutor should *never* give a talk to students; after all, the tutor probably has the privilege of many years of experience working within the subject area and this must be shared with students. Further, there are times when large classroom discussions provide a beneficial arena to share ideas and reconstruct theory. However, it is useful to combine these two pedagogical strategies with other effective approaches. Small group discussions, for instance, enable the students with less confidence to test out their ideas before exposing them to a large group. Small groups provide the opportunity for all the students to contribute in the classroom under more intimate conditions. The students may then share their understandings and ideas with the whole class as a representation of their *group* rather than as *individuals*, which feels less intimidating.

Access tutors should also employ activity work in their pedagogical practices. Such work involves small groups of students working together on a specific task. It enables students to develop their ideas and to practise and deconstruct key concepts. They may be asked to focus on a specific piece of text in relation to a series of questions, for instance. The students may identify their own sets of questions to probe in relation to the text. As another example, they may be asked to construct their own group definitions of solutions or approaches to a particular issue or problem. The group activity helps to sharpen students' individual reading skills and promotes other skills, including note-taking, problem-solving, critical thinking and analysis. It provides opportunities to collaboratively deconstruct and refashion ideas and meanings which can then be shared with the others in the classroom.

The combination of journal writing, critical reading, small and large group discussions and activity work enables students to contribute interactively to meaning making in their classrooms. Together, tutors and students can move back and forth from abstract concepts to specific examples and personal experiences to make sense of and challenge dominant canons and theories. In collaboration, they can reflexively evaluate their classroom practices, addressing power relations, inclusions and exclusions and the production of knowledge through pedagogical processes.

Access students

The classroom may be an intimidating place for access students who have had negative experiences of learning in the past. They may feel that they come to the classroom without much experience or knowledge that is valuable. This assumption must be contested; in terms of both the students' own sense of self and of wider social assumptions. Access students bring to their classrooms a wealth of resources that are a consequence of their experiences of multiple social arenas: home, family, work, health and illness, popular culture, politics, music, literature, sports and so on. These experiences represent a rich set of resources for engaging with and challenging the production of knowledge through the academic world.

Educational participation requires students to understand abstract theories. Yet these theories, when grounded in practice and experience, are not only easier to comprehend but are also of greater value. Access students should draw on their experiences to understand and challenge the theories they are presented with in the classroom. All knowledge is socially constructed, partial and situated in particular historical, cultural and geographical contexts. This means that all knowledges are open to question, particularly those that reproduce social inequalities and exclusions. It is the right of access students to test theories according to their experiences, values and perspectives, in order to critique and reconstruct them in a way that places their accounts and interests at the centre of knowledge production in the academy.

Access students need to position themselves as active learners rather than passive pupils. This demands organisation, preparation and commitment. Access students should, for example, read texts critically before seminar meetings so they can contribute to the collaborative analysis and deconstruction of these texts. The deconstruction of texts is developed through discussion and activity work with other students and through asking questions of the tutor. Such approaches lead to the collaborative *reconstruction* of social meaning against hegemonic discourses that perpetuate social exclusion.

Developing support mechanisms with other students is therefore important. This begins in the classroom, where it is crucial to respect different points of view, while supportively challenging hegemonic discourses that serve to maintain social injustices. Sharing ideas in discussions helps to sharpen understanding and analytical skills and enables each student to take a central position in the production of knowledge in the classroom.

Student support groups should be organised, wherever possible, to discuss readings, coursework or examinations. This aids learning and combats competitive and exclusive classroom practices. Meeting outside the formal classroom provides a host of opportunities. Students can help each other to grasp complex ideas, deconstruct texts and develop critical analysis. They can discuss their course and bring any problems or concerns to the tutor's attention in order to improve classroom practices – problems concerning power relations in the classroom, for example. Furthermore, students can use support groups to discuss and highlight the experiences of being a mature student, to encourage one another to face the challenge of change and to organise coalitions against institutional discrimination. Establishing coalitions will enable students to support each other through common and different experiences of injustice and to identify strategies to mobilise counter-hegemonic discourses and practices in access education.

Accessing possibilities

Collaboration between all the players involved in widening participation is the key to combating educational exclusion. This requires that students' critiques and insights are valued as highly as the contributions of academics and policy makers. Together we must deconstruct dominant discourses that serve to reproduce the cultural and structural dimensions of social injustice and replace them with discourses about inclusive education that addresses diversity. It is important that discussions between students, practitioners and academics take the form of collaborative critical inquiry. As Mary Stuart so eloquently argues:

> We need to continue to fight for individuals and communities who are not considered to have the right to define their own knowledge. It is not about widening participation in higher education simply for the self-improvement or greater inclusion of the masses, it is more radical than that. It is about challenging the academy to allow active participation from a wide range of communities and individuals who will help to redefine the parameters of higher education itself. (Stuart, 2000: 33)

Access education is a site of struggle over *meaning* and there must be the possibility for the creation of new radical discourses through collaboration with access students. Research that places students at the centre of critical inquiry produces knowledge that is grounded in their accounts and critiques and these are crucial. Access students have important things to say about their experiences and if these rich contributions are ignored, we cannot achieve the goals of social justice that should underpin access education. Interactive discussion between everyone involved in access education is needed to address the limitations and successes of current policy and practice in light of the experiences of access students and practitioners. We need to understand the institutional, discursive and policy constraints that exacerbate social exclusion and inequality so we can challenge them. Destabilising unequal power relations requires a reflexive examination of the ways we are ourselves implicated in the very social inequalities we seek to challenge.

Widening participation requires flexible approaches to research and pedagogy, which are responsive to the diverse contexts of access education. It is time to reclaim the radical politics of the access movement, challenge unequal relations of power and work in collaboration with students. Access education must seek to transform the dominant discursive practices of further and higher education that maintain social exclusion (Thompson, 2000). This does not mean simply opening spaces to fit 'non-standard' students in. It requires effecting change by legitimising a diverse range of ideas, experiences, values and perspectives within the academic world.

Note

1   I am contesting the notion that the teacher should occupy an unquestioned position of authority over students. However, I do not intend to erase the possibility that alternative reformulations of authority that sit comfortably with radical subject may be useful (Kirby, 2000; Hindess, 1995). Certainly it is helpful for marginalised groups to carry authority in terms of their diverse sets of experiences and knowledges, although all claims to authority should be open to collective critique, deconstruction and reconstruction.

Bibliography

Acker, S and Piper, D (Eds) (1984) *Is Higher Education Fair to Women?* Guildford: SRHE and NFER/Nelson

Alcoff, L (1988) 'Cultural feminism Versus Post-Structuralism: The Identity Crisis in Feminist Theory' in *Signs* Vol. 13(3) pp. 405-436

Anderson, V and Gardiner, J (1998) Continuing Education in the Universities: the old, the new and the future in Benn, R, Elliott, J and Whaley, P (Eds) *Educating Rita and Her Sisters: Women and Continuing Education* Leicester: NIACE

Appleby, Y (1994) 'Listening and Talking: Interactive Conversation as a Feminist Research Method in Studying the Experiences of Lesbian Women' Paper for BSA Conference 28-31 March 1994: Sexualities in Social Context, Preston

Aronowitz, S (1993) 'Paulo Freise's Radical Democratic Humanism' in McLaren, P and Leonard, P (Eds) Paulo Freise, *A Critical Encounter* London: Routledge

Aronowitz, S and Di Fazio, W (1994) *The Jobless Future* Minneapolis: University of Minnesota Press

Bagilhole, B (1994) 'Being Different is a Very Difficult Row to Hoe: Survival Strategies of Women Academics' in Davies, S, Lubelska, C and Quinn, J (Eds) *Changing the Subject; Women in Higher Education* London: Taylor and Francis

Ball, S (1987) *The Micropolitics of the School: Towards a Theory of School Organisation* London: Methuen

Ball, S (1990) *Politics and Policy Making in Education* London: Routledge

Barr, J (1999) *Liberating Knowledge; research, feminism and adult education* Leicester: NIACE

Becker, H (1971) *Sociological Work* London: Allen Lane

Bell, L (1997) 'Public and Private Meanings In Diaries: Researching Family and Childcare' in Ribbens, J and Edwards, R (Eds) *Feminist Dilemmas in Qualitative Research; Public Knowledge and Private Lives* London: Sage

Benn, R, Elliott, J and Whaley, P (1998) 'Introduction: Women and continuing education – where are we now?' in Benn, R, Elliott, J and Whaley, P (Eds) *Educating Rita and Her Sisters: Women and Continuing Education* Leicester: NIACE

Bertaux, D (1981) From the life-history approach to the transformation of sociological practice in Bertraux, D (Ed) *Biography and Society: the life-history approach in the social sciences* California: Sage Publications

Birch, M (1998) 'Re/Constructing Research Narratives: Self and Sociological Identity in Alternative Settings' in Ribbens, J and Edwards, R (Eds) *Feminist Dilemmas in Qualitative Research; Public Knowledge and Private Lives* London: Sage

Bird, F (1998) 'Women Staff and Equal Opportunities' in Benn, R, Elliott, J and Whaley, P (Eds) *Educating Rita and Her Sisters: Women and Continuing Education* Leicester: NIACE

Blackstone, T (11 March 1999) keynote address at the Launch of the QAA Recognition Scheme For Access to Higher Education; conference held at The British Academy

Blair, T (29 September 1999) 'Blair vows to set free nation's skills', an edited text of the speech made by the Prime Minister to the Labour Party conference in Bournemouth in *The Times*

Blundell, R, Dearden, L Goodman, A and Reed, H. (2000) The Returns to Higher Education: Evidence from a British Cohort *Economic Journal*, Vol. 110, F82-F99

Blundell, R, Dearden, L, Goodman, A and Reed, H (1997) *Higher Education, Employment and Earnings in Britain* Institute for Fiscal Studies

Blunkett, D, Secretary of State for Education and Employment (8 March 1999) 'Education Key To Tacking Social Exclusion – Blunkett *DfEE website* http://www.dfee.gov.uk/news/104.htlm

Britton, C and Baxter, A (1999) 'Becoming a Mature Student: gendered narratives of the self' in *Gender and Education*, Vol. 11 (2), pp. 179-193

Bryan, B, Dadzie, S and Scafe, S (1985) *Heart of the Race* London: Virago

Canaan, J (1997) 'Examining the Examination: Tracing the Effects of Pedagogic Authority on Cultural Studies Lecturers and Students' in Canaan, J and Epstein, D (Eds) *A Question of Discipline: Pedagogy, Power, and the Teaching of Cultural Studies* Colorado, USA: Westview Press

Carspecken, P F (1996) *Critical Ethnography in Educational research; a Theoretical and Practical Guide* New York and London: Routledge

Carvel, J (9 January 1999) 'Step toward private role in state schools' in *The Guardian*

Clarke, P (May 1999) key note speech at NELAF OCN conference 'The Future of Access', Holloway, London

Coats, M (1994) *Women's Education* Buckingham: SRHE and Open University Press

Coffey, A (1999) *The Ethnographic Self; Fieldwork and the Representation of Identity* London: Sage

Cohen, P (1999) 'Autobiography and the Hidden Curriculum Vitae' in Cohen, P (Ed) *Studies in Learning Regeneration*, Centre for New Ethnicities Research: University of East London

Cohen, L and Manion, L (1985 Second Edition) *Research Methods in Education* London, Sydney and Dover, New Hampshire: Croom Helm

Collins, PH (2000) 'What's Going On? Black feminist thought and the politics of postmodernism' in St. Pierre, E and Pillow, W (Eds) *Working the Ruins: Feminist Poststructural Theory and Methods in Education* London: Routledge

Connell, R W (1995) *Masculinities* Cambridge: Polity Press

Corrigan, P (1992) 'The Politics of Access Courses in the 1990s' in *Journal of Access Studies*, Vol. 7 (1), pp. 19-32

Davies, B (1997) The Subject of Post-structuralism: a reply to Alison Jones in *Gender and Education*, Vol. 9 (3), pp. 271-283

Davies, CA (1999) *Reflexive Ethnography: a guide to researching selves and others* London: Routledge

Davies, C and Holloway, P (1995) 'Troubling Transformation: Gender Regimes and Organizational Culture in the Academy' in Morley, L. and Walsh, V. (Eds) *Feminist Academics; Creative Agents for Change* London: Taylor and Francis

Davies, P, Williams, J and Webb, S (1997) 'Access to Higher Education in the Late Twentieth Century: Policy, Power and Discourse' in Williams, J (Ed) *Negotiating Access to Higher Education: The Discourse of Selectivity and Equity* Buckingham: The Society for Research into Higher Education and Open University Press

Dawe, R (April 1999) 'Lifelong Learning in Colleges and Universities' in *DfEE website* UK Lifelong Learning, http.//www.dfee.gov.uk

DfEE (February 1998) *The Learning Age; a renaissance for a new Britain* London: The Stationery Office

DfEE (February 1998 – booklet) *The Learning Age; a renaissance for a new Britain* London: The Stationery Office

DfEE (11 March 1999) Human Capital the Key to Business Future – Blunkett in News, *DfEE website*, http.//www.dfee.gov.uk/news

DfEE (June 1999) *Learning to Succeed – a new framework for post-16 learning* London: Stationery Office

Diamond, J (1999) 'Access: The year 2000 and beyond – what next?' *Journal of Access and Credit Studies* Summer 1999, pp. 183-191

Dockery, G (2000) 'Participatory Research: Whose roles, whose responsibilities?' in Truman, C, Mertens, D and Humphries, B (Eds) *Research and Inequality* London: UCL Press

Egerton, M and Halsey, A H (1993) 'Trends by Social Class and Gender in Access to Higher Education in Britain' in *Oxford Review of Education*, Vol. 19 (2), pp. 183-196

Ellsworth, E (1992) 'Why Doesn't This Feel Empowering? Working Through the Repressive Myths of Critical Pedagogy' in Luke, C and Gore, J (eds) *Feminisms and Critical Pedagogy* London and New York: Routledge

Ellsworth, E (1997) *Teaching Positions: difference, pedagogy and the power of address* New York, London: Teachers' College Press

Elsdon, K with Reynolds, J and Stewart, S (1995) *Voluntary Organisations: citizenship, learning and change* Leicester: NIACE

Epstein, D (1991) *Changing Classroom Cultures: An Examination of Anti-Racist Pedagogy, INSET and School Change in the Context of Local and National Politics* unpublished PhD thesis; University of Birmingham

Epstein, D (1993) *Changing Classroom Cultures; Anti-racism, politics and schools* Stoke-on-Trent: Trentham Books

Epstein, D (1995) 'In Our (New) Right Minds' in Morley, L and Walsh, V (Eds) *Feminist Academics; Creative Agents for Change* London: Taylor and Francis

Epstein, D (1997) 'The Voice of Authority: On Lecturing in Cultural Studies' in Canaan, J and Epstein, D (Eds) *A Question of Discipline: Pedagogy, Power, and the Teaching of Cultural Studies* Colorado, USA: Westview Press

Equal Opportunities Commission (2000) *Valuing Women: The Campaign for Equal Pay* www.eoc.org.uk

Evans, M (1995) 'Ivory Towers: Life in the Mind' in Morley, L and Walsh, V (Eds) *Feminist Academics; Creative Agents for Change* London: Taylor and Francis

Field, J (1999) 'Is Recruitment to Access Courses Rising or Falling?' in *Access Networking* Spring 1999 Number 7

Fieldhouse, R (1996) 'Historical and Political Context', 'The Nineteenth Century' and 'An Overview of British Adult Education in the Twentieth Century' in Fieldhouse, R (Ed) *A History of Modern British Adult Education* Leicester: NIACE

Fielding, N (1993) 'Ethnography' in Gilbert, N (Ed) *Researching Social Life* London: Sage

Flax, J (1995) 'Postmodernism and Gender Relations in Feminist Theory' in Blair, Holland with Sheldon (Eds) *Identity and Diversity; Gender and the Experience of Education* Avon: Open University

Foucault, M (1979) *The History of Sexuality, Volume 1, An Introduction* (translated from the French by Robert Hurley) London: Allen Lane

Foucault, M (1975) *Discipline and Punish: The Birth of the Prison* translated from the French by Alan Sheridan, London: Allen Lane

Foucault, M (1984) 'The Means of Correct Training' (from Discipline and Punish) in Paul Rabinow (ed) *The Foucault Reader* London: Penguin Books

Foucault, M (1986) *The History of Sexuality, Volume Two, The Use of Pleasure* Harmondsworth: Viking

Fraser, N (1997) *Justice Interruptus: Critical Reflections on the 'Postsocialist' Condition* London: Routledge

Freire, P (1972) *Pedagogy of the Oppressed* Harmondsworth: Penguin

Fryer, R (1990) 'The Challenge to Working Class Education' in Simon, B (Ed) *The Search for Enlightenment: the working class and adult education in the twentieth century* London: Lawrence and Wishart

Gardiner, J and O'Rourke, R (1998) 'Women's Career Progression: a Case Study' in Benn, R, Elliott, J and Whaley, P (eds) *Educating Rita and Her Sisters; women and continuing education* Leicester: NIACE

Giddens, A (1998) *The Third Way: The Renewal of Social Democracy* Cambridge: Polity Press

Gore, J (1993) *The Struggle for Pedagogies: Critical and Feminist Discourses as Regimes of Truth* London: Routledge

Green, P and Webb, S (1997) 'Student Voices: Alternative Routes, Alternative Identities in Williams, J (Ed) *Negotiating Access to Higher Education; The Discourse of Selectivity and Equity* Buckingham: SHRE and Open University Press

Griffiths, M (1998) *Educational Research for Social Justice getting off the fence* Buckingham: Open University Press

Grimshaw and Rubery (2001) *The Gender Pay Gap: a research review* Equal Opportunities Commisision

Hall, S (1992) 'Introduction: Identity in Question' in Hall, S, Held, D and McGrew, T (Eds) *Modernity and Its Futures* Cambridge: Polity Press

Hanmer, J (1997) 'Women and Reproduction' in Richardson, D and Robinson, V (Eds) *Introducing Women's Studies* Hampshire and London: Macmillan Press

Harding, S (1991) *Whose Science? Whose Knowledge?* Buckingham: Open University Press

Hart, M (1992) *Working and Educating for Life; Feminist and International Perspectives on Adult Education* London: Routledge

Hernàndez, A (1997) *Pedagogy, Democracy and Feminism: Rethinking the public sphere* New York: State University of New York Press

Hey, V (1996) ''A Game of Two Halves' – A Critique of Some Complicities: between hegemonic and counter-hegemonic discourses concerning marketisation and education' in *Discourse: studies in the cultural politics of education*, Vol. 17 (3), pp. 351-362

Hey, V (1997) *The Company She Keeps* Buckingham: Open University Press

Hey, V (2000) 'Troubling the Auto/biography of the Questions: Re/thinking Rapport and the Politics of Social Class in Feminist Participant Observation' in *Genders and Sexuality in Educational Ethnography*, Vol. 3, pp. 161-183

Hindess, B (1995) 'Great Expectations: freedom and authority' *Oxford Literary Review* 17, pp. 29-49

Hodgson, A (2000) 'The challenge of widening participation in lifelong learning' in Hodgson, A (Ed) *Policies, Politics and the Future of Lifelong Learning* London: Kogan Page

Holland, C with Frank, F and Cooke, T (1998) *Literacy and the New Work Order, an international literature review* Leicester: NIACE

Hoyle, E (1982) 'Micropolitics of educational organisations' in *Educational Management and Administration*, Vol. 10, pp. 87-98

Jackson, S (1997) 'Women, Marriage and Family Relationships' in Richardson, D and Robinson, V (Eds) *Introducing Women's Studies* Hampshire and London: Macmillan Press

155

Johnson, R (1997) 'Teaching Without Guarantees: Cultural Studies, Pedagogy, and Identity' in Canaan, J and Epstein, D (Eds) *A Question of Discipline: Pedagogy, Power, and the Teaching of Cultural Studies* Colorado, USA: Westview Press

Johnson-Riordan, L (1997) 'Teaching/Cultural Studies (or Pedagogy for 'World'- Travellers/'World'-Travelling Pedagogy' in Canaan, J and Epstein, D (Eds) *A Question of Discipline: Pedagogy, Power, and the Teaching of Cultural Studies* Colorado, USA: Westview Press

Jones, A (1993) 'Becoming a 'Girl': post-structuralist suggestions for educational research' in *Gender and Education*, Vol. 5 (2), pp. 157-165

Jones, K (1999) 'In the Shadow of the Centre-Left: post-conservative politics and rethinking educational change' in *Discourse: studies in the cultural politics of education*, Vol. 20 (2), pp. 235-247

Kelly, L, Burton, S and Regan, L (1994) 'Researching Women's Lives or Studying Women's Oppression? Reflections on what Constitutes Feminist Research' in Maynard, M and Purvis, J (Eds) (1994) *Researching Women's Lives from a Feminist Perspective* London: Taylor and Francis

Kennedy, H (1997) *Learning Works* The Further Education Funding Council

Kennedy, M and Piette, B (1991) 'From the Margins to the Mainstream: Issues around Women's Studies on Adult Education and Access Courses' in Aaron, J and Walby, S (Eds) *Out of the Margins* London, New York and Philadelphia: Falmer Press

Kenway, J (1995) 'Feminist Theories of the State: To Be or Not To Be' in Blair, Holland with Sheldon (Eds) *Identity and Diversity; Gender and the Experience of Education* Avon: Open University

Kenway, J and Epstein, D (1996) 'Introduction: the marketisation of school education: feminist studies and perspectives' in *Discourse: studies in the cultural politics of education*, Vol. 17 (3)

Kenway, J, Willis, S, Blackmore, J and Rennie, L (1994) 'Making 'Hope Practical' Rather than 'Despair Convincing': feminist post-structuralism, gender reform and educational change' in *British Journal of Sociology of Education*, Vol. 15 (2), pp. 187-210

Kirby, V (2000) 'Response to Jane Gallop's 'The Teacher's breasts' in Johnson, L, Lee, A and Green, B 'The Ph.D. and the Autonomous Self: gender, rationality and postgraduate pedagogy' *Studies in Higher Education*, Vol. 25 (2)

Kirton, A (1999) 'Lessons from Access Education' in Hayton, A (Ed) *Tackling Disaffection and Social Exclusion: Education Perspectives and Policies* London: Kogan Page

Kuhn, A (1995) *Family Secrets: Acts of Memory and Imagination* London: Verso

Lather, P (1991) *Getting Smart; Feminist Research and Pedagogy With/in the Postmodern* London and New York: Routledge

Law, C (1998) 'Accrediting Women, Normalising Women' in Benn, R, Elliott, J and Whaley, P (Eds) *Educating Rita and Her Sisters: Women and Continuing Education* Leicester: NIACE

156

Lawrence, M (1987) 'Education and Identity: The Social Origins of Anorexia' in Lawrence, M (Ed) *Fed Up and Hungry; Women, Oppression and Food* London: The Women's Press

Leonard, M (1994) 'Transforming the Household;: Mature Women Students and Access to Higher Education' in Davies, S, Lubelska, C and Quinn, J (Eds) *Changing the Subject; Women in Higher Education* London: Taylor and Francis

Lothian Anti Poverty Alliance (February 2001) 'Poverty in the UK' http://www.lapa.org.uk/Poverty/Statistics/UK

www.lapa.org.uk/Poverty/Statistics/UK

Lucas, N, Betts, D, Derrick, J, Evans, D, Guile, D, Spours, K and Macwhinnie, I (1997) *Policy and Management Issues for Incorporated Colleges*, Working Paper Number 21, Post-16 Education Centre, Institute of Education University of London

Lucey, H (3 July 2000) 'Girls Growing Up in Late Modernity' [provisional title], paper presented at *Education for Social Democracies* conference, Culture, Communication and Societies, Institute of Education, University of London

Luke, C and Gore, J (1992) 'Women in the Academy: Strategy, Struggle and Survival' in Luke, C and Gore, J (eds) *Feminisms and Critical Pedagogy* London and New York: Routledge

Mac an Ghaill, M and Haywood, C (1997) 'The End of Anti-oppressive education? A Differentialist Critique' in *International Studies in Sociology of Education*, Vol. 7 (1), pp. 21-34

Magezis, J (1996) *Teach Yourself Women's Studies* London: Hoddder Headline

Maher, F A and Tetreault, M (1994) *The Feminist Classroom* New York: Basic Books

Major, L E (16 May 2000) 'So who gets the job?' in The Guardian Higher Education

Major, L E (27 October 1998) 'Learning Derailed' in *The Guardian Higher Education*

Marrin, Minette (November 1999) 'What we must learn about selecting undergraduates' in *The Daily Telegraph*

Mauthner, M (1998a) Kindred Spirits: Stories of Sister relationships (unpublished PhD dissertation), Institute of Education University of London

Mauthner, M (1998b) 'Bringing Silent Voices into a Public Discourse; Researching Accounts of Sister Relationships' in Ribbens, J and Edwards, R (eds) (1998) *Feminist Dilemmas in Qualitative Research; Public Knowledge and Private Lives* London, New Delhi and Thousand Oaks: Sage

Mauthner, M and Hey, V (1999) 'Researching Girls: post-structuralist approach' in *Educational and Child Psychology*, Vol. 16 (2), pp. 67-84

Maynard, M and Purvis, J (Eds) (1994) *Researching Women's Lives from a Feminist Perspective* London: Taylor and Francis

Mayo, M (1997) *Imagining Tomorrow: Adult Education for Transformation* Leicester: NIACE

Maxwell, B (1996) 'Open College Networks; Are They Still for Adult Learners?' *Adults Learning* January 1996, pp. 111-112

McGivney, V (1998) 'Dancing into the future' in Benn, R, Elliott, J and Whaley, P (Eds) *Educating Rita and Her Sisters* Leicester: NIACE

Merrill, B (1996) "I'm Doing Something for Myself": Mature Women Students in Universities" in Hill, S and Merrill, B (Eds) *Access, Equity, Participation and Organisational Change* Department of Continuing Education, University of Warwick, Faculte de Psychologie et des Sciences de l'Education, Universite Catholique de Louvan and ESREA

Mies, M (1986) *Patriarchy and Accumulation on a World Scale: Women in the International Division of Labour* London: Zed Books

Miller, J (1997) *Autobiography and Research* University of London Institute of Education Chicago, March 1997

Morley, L (1999) *Organising Feminisms: The Micropolitics of the Academy* Hampshire: Macmillan Press

Moss, W (1987) *Breaking the Barriers: Eight Case Studies of Women Returning to Learning in North London* London: REPLAN and Access to Learning for Adults

National Open College Network (1997-1998) *Annual Report* Derby: NOCN

National Open College Network (2000) *Lifelong Learning and the Recognition of Achievement: A Position Statement of the National Open College Network* Derby: NOCN website www.nocn.ac.uk

Nicolson, P (1997) 'Motherhood and Women's Lives' in Richardson, D and Robinson, V (Eds) *Introducing Women's Studies* Hampshire and London: Macmillan Press

Oakley, A (1990) 'Who's afraid of the randomised controlled trial? Some dilemmas of the scientific method and 'good' research practice' in Roberts (Ed) *Women's Health Counts* London: Routledge

O'Malley, B (27 June 1997) *Educate to Liberate* Features and Arts website

Orner, M (1992) 'Interrupting the Calls for Student Voice in 'Liberatory' Education: A Feminist Poststructuralist Perspective' in Luke, C and Gore, J (Eds) *Feminisms and Critical Pedagogy* London: Routledge

Pascall, G and Cox, R (1993) Women Returning to Higher Education Buckingham: SRHE and Open University Press

Paulston, R (2000) 'Imagining comparative education: past, present and future' *Compare*, Vol. 30 (3), pp. 353-368

Pearson, R (1998) 'Nimble Fingers revisited': reflections on women and Third World industrialisation in the late twentieth century' in Jackson, C and Pearson (Eds) *Feminist Visions of Development: Gender Analysis and Policy* London: Routledge

Power, S and Whitty, G (1999) 'New Labour's Educational Policy' in *Journal of Educational Policy* London: Taylor and Francis, pp. 535-546

Purvis, J (1987) 'Social Class, education and ideals of femininity' in Arnot, M and Weiner, G (Eds) *Gender and the Politics of Schooling* London: Unwin Hyman in association with the Open University

Purvis, J (1991) *A History of Women's Education in England* Buckingham: Open University Press

Rabinow, P (Ed) (1984) *The Foucault Reader* London: Penguin Books

Ramazanoglu, C and Holland, J (1999) 'Tripping Over Experience: some problems in feminist epistemology' in *Discourse: studies in cultural politics of education*, Vol. 20 (3), pp. 381-391

Randall, J (11 March 1999) keynote address at the Launch of the QAA Recognition Scheme For Access to Higher Education; conference held at The British Academy

Reay, D (1998) *Class Work; Mothers' Involvement in their Children's Primary Schooling* London: UCL Press, Taylor and Francis

Reich, R (1992) *The Work of Nations* New York: Vintage Books

Ribbens, J and Edwards, R (Eds) (1998) *Feminist Dilemmas in Qualitative Research; Public Knowledge and Private Lives* London, New Delhi and Thousand Oaks: Sage

Robinson, V (1997 second edition) 'Introducing Women's Studies' in Richardson, D and Robinson, V (Eds) *Introducing Women's Studies* Hampshire and London: Macmillan Press

Rosen, V (1990) *Beyond Higher Education: A Survey and Analysis of the Experience of Access Students Proceeding Through the Polytechnic of North London and into Employment* London: Access to Learning for Adults

Ryan, A (2000) 'Peripherality, solidarity and mutual learning in the global/local development business' in Thompson, J (Ed) *Stretching the Academy: The politics and practice of widening participation in Higher Education* Leicester: NIACE

Sand, B (1998) 'Lifelong Learning: vision, policy and practice' in *Journal of Access and Credit Studies*, Winter 1998, pp. 17-39

Sand, B, Donnelly, E and Sanders, J (1999) Editorial in *Access Networking* Spring 1999, Number 7

Sellers, J (1998) 'Juggling for a living: the working lives of women adult education tutors' in Benn, R, Elliott, J, and Whaley, P (eds) *Educating Rita and Her Sisters* Leicester:NIACE

Sherman, J (13 January 1999) 'No cash for those who refuse jobs; 'Workfare' testing for state benefits' in *The Times*

Shuster, M (1994) 'Transforming the Curriculum' in Davies, S, Lubelska, C and Quinn, J (Eds) *Changing the Subject; Women in Higher Education* London: Taylor and Francis

159

Skeggs, B (1994) 'Situating the Production of Feminist Ethnography' in

Maynard, M and Purvis, J (Eds) *Researching Women's Lives from a Feminist Perspective* London: Taylor and Francis

Skeggs, B (1995a) 'Women's Studies in Britain in the 1990s: Entitlement Cultures and Institutional Constraints' in *Women's Studies International Forum* Vol. 18(4), pp. 475-485

Skeggs, B (1995b) 'Theorising, ethics and representation in feminist ethnography' in Skeggs (ed) *Feminist Cultural Theory: Process and Production* Manchester: Manchester University Press

Skeggs, B (1997) *Formations of Class and Gender* London: Sage

Spours, K and Lucas, N (July 1996) 'The Formation of a National Sector of Incorporated Colleges: Beyond the FEFC Model' Working Paper Number 19, Post-16 Education Centre, Institution of Education, University of London

Standing, K (1999) 'Lone Mothers' Involvement in their Children's Schooling: towards a new typology of maternal involvement' in *Gender and Education,* Vol. 11 (1), pp. 57-73

Stanley, J (1995) 'Pain(t) for Healing: The Academic Conference and the Classed/ Embodied Self' in Morley, L and Walsh, V (Eds) *Feminist Academics; Creative Agents for Change* London: Taylor and Francis

Stanley, L (1992) *The Auto/biographical I the theory and practice of feminist auto/ biography* Manchester and New York: Manchester University Press

Stanley, L (1993) 'On autobiographies in sociology' in *Sociology,* Vol. 27 (1), pp. 41-52

Stanley, L and Wise, S (New Edition 1993, first published 1983) *Breaking Out Again* London and New York: Routledge

Stuart, M (2000) 'Beyond Rethoric: reclaiming a radical agenda for active participation in higher education' in Thompson, J (Ed) *Stretching the Academy: The politics and practice of widening participation in Higher Education* Leicester: NIACE

Stuart, N (April 1999) 'An overview of lifelong learning' on *DfEE website* UK Lifelong Learning

Tamboukou, M (1999) 'Spacing Herself: women in education' in *Gender and Education,* Vol. 11 (2), pp. 125-139

Taylor-Gooby, P (September 28, 1999) 'Opportunity Knocks' in *The Guardian*

Thompson, A (1997) 'Gatekeeping: Inclusionary and Exclusionary Discourses and Practices' in Williams, J (Ed) *Negotiating Access to Higher Education: The Discourse of Selectivity and Equity* Buckingham: The Society for Research into Higher Education and Open University Press

Thompson, J (2000) 'Introduction' in Thompson, J (Ed) *Stretching the Academy: The politics and practice of widening participation in Higher Education* Leicester: NIACE

Tight, M (1993) 'Access, not access courses: Maintaining a broad vision' in Edward, R, Siemenski, S and Zeldin, D (Eds) *Adult Learners, Education and Training* Buckinghamshire: Open University Press

Uden, T (1996) *Widening Participation: Routes to a Learning Society: a policy discussion* Leicester: NIACE

Usher, R (1997) 'Telling a Story about Research and Research as Story-telling: Postmodern Approaches to Social Research' in McKenzie, G and Powell, D and Usher, R (Eds) *Understanding Social Research: Perspectives on Methodology and Practice* London: Falmer Press

Walkerdine, V (1987) 'Sex, power and pedagogy' in Arnot, M and Weiner, G (Eds) *Gender and the Politics of Schooling* London: Unwin Hyman

Walter, N (1998) *The New Feminism* London: Little Brown and Company

Webb, S (1997) 'Alternative Students? Conceptualizations of Difference' in Williams, J (Ed) *Negotiating Access to Higher Education; the Discourse of Selectivity and Equity* Buckingham: SHRHE and Open University Press

Weedon, C (1997 second edition) *Feminist Practice and Poststructuralist Theory* Oxford: Blackwell

Weiler, K (1994) 'Freire and a feminist pedagogy of difference' in McLaren, P and Lankshear, C (Eds) *Politics of Liberation* London: Routledge

White, M (28 September 1999) 'Blair's new moral agenda' in *The Guardian*

Wicks, M (2000) Keynote address to Universities Association of Continuing Education Conference

Williams, J (1997a) 'The Discourse of Access: The Legitimisation of Selectivity' in Williams, Jenny (Ed) *Negotiating Access to Higher Education: The Discourse of Selectivity and Equity* Buckingham: The Society for Research into Higher Education and Open University Press

Williams, Jenny (1997b) 'Institutional Rhetorics and Realities' in Williams, Jenny (Ed) *Negotiating Access to Higher Education: The Discourse of Selectivity and Equity* Buckingham: The Society for Research into Higher Education and Open University Press

Williams, J (1997c) 'Conclusions' in Williams, J (Ed) *Negotiating Access to Higher Education; the Discourse of Selectivity and Equity* Buckingham: SHRHE and Open University Press

Willis, P (1977) *Learning to Labour* Farnborough: Saxon House

Woodrow, M (1996) 'Access is not obsolete', *The Lecturer*, February

Woolf, V (1994, first published 1929) *A Room of One's Own* London: Flamingo

Young, M (1999) 'Some Reflections on the Concepts of Social Exclusion and Inclusion: Beyond the Third Way' in Hayton, A (Ed) *Tackling Disaffection and Social Exclusion* London: Kogan Page

Index

access education: history of, 7-8, 14-15, 64-65; policy contexts, 20-26; and self-discovery, 100-103, 140; and social justice, 8, 10, 21, 36, 107, 113, 142

Access to Higher Education, 7, 15, 17, 18-19, 25, 64, 117-118

autobiography, 4-7, 9; as method, 49-51; as pedagogical tool, 69-71

citizenship, 28, 30, 62-63, 104-105, 137, 140, 141

collaboration, 10, 45-48, 141, 147; collaborative methods and methodology, 39-54, 125; pedagogy, 46, 58, 135-136; reflexivity, 39-40

data analysis, 51-53

deconstruction, 3, 9, 19, 36, 83, 107, 136-138, 146, 147

discourse, 2, 13; neo-liberal discourse, 14, 26, 34, 58, 100-102, 104; positioned discourse and shifting positions discourse, 98, 108-111; radical discourses, 2, 14, 112-116, 117-132, 141, 142; of widening educational participation, 20, 36, 62-63, 137-138, 140-141; of working-class women, 83-84, 109-111

Ellsworth, Elizabeth, 57-58

empowerment, 86-89, 131

Epstein, Debbie, 71-72, 79-80, 82-83, 86

ethical issues, 43-45, 52-53

ethnography, 15; and feminist post-structuralism, 40-43

experience, 2, 9, 41-42, 129-130, 146

Feminism, 3, 6, 8, 42, 49, 56, 58-62, 120, 131-132, 142; feminist post-structuralism, 8, 10, 39, 40-42, 53, 58-59, 87, 102

Foucault, Michel, 2, 90-91, 109, 121-122

Freire, Paulo, 46, 55-56, 75

Further Education Lecturers, 22, 34-35

Giddens, Anthony, 27-30, 31

Hall, Stuart, 98-99, 115

Hart, Mechthild, 30-33

hegemony, definition of, 2

Housewifization of labour, 30-33, 137

identity formation, 98; identification, 98-99

intimidating education, 77-78, 138; and examinations, 89-94; 139-140

'juggling', 35-36

Kennedy, Helena, 19, 20-21

Lather, Patti, 8, 39-40

The Learning Age, 22-24

Learning to Succeed, 24-26

Learning Works, 20-22

masculinity, 105-107

mass education, 78-81

Mauthner, Melanie, 49, 98

meritocracy, 28-30, 140

micro-politics, 118-119, 125, 127, 142-143
Morley, Louise, 87, 118-119

New Deal, 25, 27, 28

Open College Network, 18, 19, 20, 66-67

pedagogy, 4; critical, 55-58; feminist, 56; feminist post-structural critiques, 57-62; interactive, 71-74, 144; research as a pedagogical tool, 69, 136
positionality, 8, 98-99, 111
power: and feminist methodology, 44; and classroom inequalities, 47; power relations, 27, 44, 46-48, 53-54, 59, 88, 120, 125, 139, 148; vulnerability in research, 44-45
praxis, 8, 142
progress and success: dominant notions, 102, 107, 116, 141

reflexivity, 9, 40, 61, 118, 139, 144
research relationships, 42-43, 136
Return to Study, 17, 18, 115, 120
risk-society, 29-30, 31-32, 35, 36, 137-138

selection: as exclusionary process, 84-85, 101, 138, 140
Skeggs, Beverly, 5-6; 43-44, 81, 131
social aspects of learning, 24, 70, 72
standards and standardisation, 65-69, 92, 138; and notions of transparency, 65-66
strategies for widening participation, 143- 147
student voice, 58-59
subjectivity, 3, 98; as shifting, 97-116, 140-141

Third Way politics, 26-30; reform welfare state, 27; and risk, 29-30, 31-32; and social exclusion, 28

Walkerdine, Valerie, 59
Williams, Jenny, 14, 80-81, 85, 138
women's access to education, 78-79; woman-only provision, 128-129;
Women's Studies, 19, 129-131
women's work: marginal labour, 32-35, 141